THE FUSS-FREE TODDLER COOKBOOK

THE FUSS-FREE
TODDLER
COOKBOOK

Mealtimes Made Easy with Healthy Recipes for the Whole Family

Barbara Lamperti

PHOTOGRAPHY BY BIZ JONES

**ROCKRIDGE
PRESS**

For general information on our other products and services or to obtain technical support, please contact our Customer Care Department within the United States at (866) 744-2665, or outside the United States at (510) 253-0500.

Rockridge Press publishes its books in a variety of electronic and print formats. Some content that appears in print may not be available in electronic books, and vice versa.

Interior and Cover Designer: Brian Lewis
Art Producer: Sue Bischofberger
Editor: Ada Fung
Production Editor: Ruth Sakata Corley

Photography © 2019 Biz Jones
Author photo courtesy of Eva Simone Photography

ISBN: Print 978-1-64611-005-6 | eBook 978-1-64611-006-3

R0

To Albert. Your love and support made it happen.

To Alex, Luca, and Nonna MG. Love you 3000.

Contents

Introduction ix

1 FEEDING YOUR TODDLER WITHOUT THE FUSS 1

2 NOT-JUST-MUFFINS BREAKFAST 31

3 HANDHELDS FOR LITTLE HANDS 47

4 VEGETABLES YOUR KIDS WILL (MIGHT) EAT 63

5 FISH STICK—FREE SEAFOOD MEALS 79

6 NON-NUGGET CHICKEN DINNERS 97

7 BEYOND THE MEATBALL MEATY MAINS 115

8 JUST ADD THIS: DIPS, SAUCES, AND SPREADS 133

Measurement Conversions 145
Resources 146
Index 149

Beef and Zucchini Baked
Samosas, page 56

Introduction

When I got married, the very first thing I bought with my husband was a dining table with chairs. I could live without a couch or TV or closet, but not without a dining table.

I grew up in Italy, where the kitchen was the heart of the house. Our family enjoyed many lunches and every dinner together at the kitchen table. It was a relaxing time (cell phones did not exist and watching TV during meals was not allowed), a time to enjoy food and share the daily news. When I got married, I really wanted to share this family tradition with my new husband, Albert, and when we had kids, it became even more important. Early on, with just me and my hubby, meals were simple and romantic. Albert is a food lover and very into healthy and simple food. I cooked and he set the table and washed the dishes. When Luca arrived, and then Alex, meals became . . . trickier.

I knew how to cook for adults, but what about cooking for a baby or a toddler?

Combining the baby's schedule with my work schedule was not easy (meaning: late dinners). In the beginning, it really looked like I would need to prepare different meals for each member of the family and serve them at different times, basically restaurant-style. And I'm not even mentioning the fact that cooking while taking care of a baby or toddler requires the skills (and arms) of an octopus!

Figuring out how to prepare family meals without stress was not easy, and, yes, I cannot count the number of times I offered my hubby a lovely "soup" for dinner—our baby's vegetable purée in a bigger cup—or the many times I ended up cooking completely different things for each family member. That's three times the work and three times the mess, which was stressful, tiring, and definitely not even close to the "happy family around the table eating the same meal" idea that I had in mind.

So, I made a big decision: no more à la carte menus. I would make only one family meal that (hopefully) would please both the little ones and the big ones. After much thought on how to accomplish this, I decided to "toddlerize" my adult recipes, basically adjusting the meals my husband and I had been eating all along to be appealing and tasty for the kids, too. When I say "toddlerize," I don't mean spending a ton of time making the food look fancy and cute on the plate. I understand that kids really like eating food that looks adorable, but I was trying to spend less time in the kitchen—not more!

My idea of "toddlerizing" mostly means resizing (cutting food into small pieces), reshaping (cutting a cherry tomato diagonally and flipping it to become a heart), adding ingredients (grating zucchini into meatballs, or topping a dish with cheese), skipping ingredients (leaving out the spicy stuff that adults can add to their own portions), reducing ingredients (using half the amount of a strong-flavored spice—the flavor will be there but will not be overwhelming for little taste buds), changing the texture (the immersion blender will be your friend), switching the cooking method (baking instead of steaming), or adding colors (half a small cooked beet stirred into a pancake batter for a fun pink color). The idea is to make simple changes that will get little ones interested and willing to try their food.

In this book, I'm happy to share with you my delicious discoveries—healthy, organic, and tasty recipes that have been "toddlerized" with special tips, suggestions, and tweaks that make each one enjoyable for the whole family.

May you embrace the warmth and togetherness of a family meal. *Buon Appetito!*

1

FEEDING YOUR TODDLER WITHOUT THE FUSS

Imagine a kitchen table with a rascally baby in a high chair looking curiously at big brother and sister as they laugh while their parents ask them funny questions about their day. It's dinner time, there's one meal on the table, and no one is fussing. Is this too perfect to be real?

I can't promise you that every family meal will be Instagram-perfect, but I can share my tips for making the family meal as stress-free as possible for your family. The focus should always be on the quality time spent together, rather than a battle over who won't eat what. I believe in serving one meal to the entire family, one that everyone will like. Maybe your kids won't try everything—or even eat much of it at all—but that's OK. The important thing is that you are presenting your kids with a variety of healthy foods—and that you're no longer stressing over cooking multiple meals. Let's start!

ONE MEAL, MULTIPLE PLATES (OR HOW TO STOP BEING A SHORT-ORDER COOK)

Family meals are an opportunity to get together and enjoy time with each other. But if your toddler fights every single bite, the fun goes away and your stress level goes up. My Luca has always been a light eater and is often suspicious of what I put in front of him, so I totally get it. We fought him at every turn and meals would end in tears (his . . . and mine).

That's why I decided to try some new approaches to feeding my toddler healthy meals. Not every tip of mine will work for your family—that's normal and perfectly fine (they don't work for me all the time, either). I suggest you try them out and find a combination of approaches that will fit your family.

It all begins with what I believe is one of the most important elements for a fuss-free meal: the whole family eating together. I know this is not always possible due to parents working late or a newborn being on a different feeding schedule. Maybe you can try to feed the baby before dinner so that they can nap or play while everyone else is eating. Or you can plan a family meal twice a week. Weekends have always been the best time for us to have meals together, so that might be a good place to start. The idea is to serve one meal, one that all members of the family can eat and enjoy. Tell your little one, "This is what mommy/daddy prepared today for the whole family. Let's eat together!" If your toddler knows that there are no options other than what has been served, they will concentrate more on choosing what they have on their plate rather than continually asking for something different.

What really worked for us was serving easy and healthy recipes that could be easily adapted to appeal to both adults and kids. Through my own trial and error—along with reader feedback from my website, BuonaPappa—I learned how to transform a recipe for adults into a toddler-friendly one, or how to "toddlerize" it. For example, I transformed fish fillets into baked fish and cauliflower croquettes coated with almond meal for extra flavor (and nutrients). When I had a few extra minutes, I shaped them into butterflies, which my kids really loved.

The end goal is to expose your toddler to a variety of healthy and tasty foods, which will ultimately make your life easier. Your children might not eat everything; that's fine. Even if they try a tiny bite of a new food, consider that a success. Exposure is the key. Every recipe in this book has been tested on my family and received a thumbs-up from both of my kids, even my lovably picky Luca.

FOOD AND TODDLERS

When Luca was born, as an Italian and a first-time mom, I didn't really know the definition of a "toddler." Only when I started shopping for baby clothes did I learn that a toddler is a child between the ages of 1 and 3. Still, that information didn't prepare me for the dramatic change in food habits that a toddler experiences.

The American Association of Pediatrics (AAP) recommends introducing solid foods to babies between 4 and 6 months of age. You can do this either by feeding them purées or by baby-led weaning, which is offering babies soft finger foods and letting them decide what to eat. There is no "best" practice. I suggest following the method that best suits you and your little one, and you can also use a mix of the two. That's what I did with my two boys. They loved super-smooth textures and being fed purées, and at the same time they had fun feeding themselves with tiny pieces of foods between meals. The "baby phase" is usually between 4 and 12 months of age. Your little one will slowly transition from your breast or the bottle to using a sippy cup and a plate or bowl, and you will be feeding your baby super-soft foods. They will need only about 1 tablespoon of food to make a meal. At this age, babies love to grab things, so feeding them with foods they can pick up and giving them a sippy cup is the easiest way to feed them.

At around 12 months of age, your baby officially transitions to toddlerhood and should be able to start eating with a baby spoon and fork. At this time, you might also want to transition from a sippy cup to a straw cup or an open cup (with your help). Using a child-safe knife comes later on, as it requires more hand-eye coordination. Just remember that every kid is different and develops at a different pace.

The recipes here are written with toddlers in mind (around 18 months), but they are easily adjustable for older and younger kids. An older kid will be able to enjoy bigger pieces and cut their meal by themselves, and an immersion blender will easily transform a recipe into a purée for kids who are not quite ready for new textures.

TODDLER NUTRITIONAL NEEDS

A toddler's basic nutritional needs are similar to those of adults—yet another reason why cooking one meal for the entire family makes sense. The following three categories are macronutrients that everyone needs in their diet and these three fundamentals should be offered to your child every day:

Complex carbohydrates from whole grains or vegetables. They are the main source of energy for our bodies.

Protein from meat, poultry, fish, nuts, legumes, or dairy. Proteins are considered the building blocks of our bodies.

Healthy fats in the form of oils (olive oil), seeds (chia, hemp, flax), nuts, eggs, avocado, and fish. This category is just as essential as the previous ones. Healthy fats are needed for proper brain development and they also contribute to the absorption, storage, and transport of fat-soluble vitamins (A, D, E, K).

Every recipe in this book incorporates a healthy balance of these macronutrients, so you can feel confident about making any of the recipes.

In addition to the basic macronutrients, there are certain nutrients and vitamins that play an essential role in a toddler's healthy mind and growing body. You will want to include these in the weekly meal routine:

Iron. A mineral found in plants and animals, iron is essential for your child's growth and development, as it carries oxygen from the lungs to the rest of the body. Without iron, tissues, muscles, and organs will not get the oxygen they need and will not be able to function. Examples of foods that are high in iron include red meat, lentils, leafy greens, beans, and eggs. These should be combined with foods rich in vitamin C for even better absorption.

Fiber. This is a carbohydrate that the body doesn't digest. For this reason, fiber is an important element of a healthy diet. It will keep your little one's bowel movements regular and prevent constipation. Fiber-rich foods include whole grains, beans, oats, broccoli, and apples.

Omega-3 fatty acids. All fats are not created equal. Certain fats like omega-3s are essential for your toddler's brain development and heart health. Examples of omega-3-rich foods are salmon, sardines, avocado, flaxseed, and nuts.

Vitamins A, B, C, D. These are all necessary for the healthy functioning of our kids' bodies. Each vitamin family has a different role and a different recommended daily intake. Vitamin C boosts our little one's immune system and helps the body resist infection. Vitamin A is important for eyesight and, like the C family, improves the immune system. The vitamin D family is important for strong bone structure and teeth because it helps the body absorb calcium. Last but not least are the B vitamins, which support the metabolism and create energy in your toddler's body.

The biggest difference between an adult meal and a toddler meal is portion size. You might be surprised by the small amount of food that a toddler really needs to grow healthy and strong. When your toddler doesn't finish the meal you serve them, you might think it's them being picky but they could just be full. The table on page 6 will give you an idea of what your toddler needs each day, but use this as a general guideline—every child is different.

Keep in mind that toddlers' appetites will vary from meal to meal and from day to day. I know it can be hard because, of course, you don't want your kids to go hungry or have an unbalanced diet, but try to think of your toddler's nutritional intake in terms of what they're getting in a week and try not to get too hung up if at one meal they ignore their vegetables entirely.

A kid's appetite is like a roller coaster. I cannot count the times I prepared a delicious, colorful, and healthy lunch box for my boys, only to see it come back untouched. A few days later, I would include the same combination of foods and their lunch box would come back empty, with both complaining that I didn't give them enough food. That's the way it goes in #lifewithkids. With time and experience, I learned not to focus on a single meal but to check the kids' daily (or even weekly) food intake. This gives me a better idea of whether or not they are eating an overall balanced diet. If your little one barely touches food at one meal, don't stress too much. Just step back and look at the big picture.

A Toddler's Daily Nutritional Needs

FOOD GROUP	SERVINGS PER DAY	EXAMPLES OF ONE SERVING
Grains	6	• 2 to 3 whole-grain crackers • ½ slice of whole-grain bread • ¼ cup cooked pasta, rice, or other grain • ¼ bun, muffin, bagel • ¼ cup dry cereal
Fruit and Vegetables	5	• ¼ cup cooked vegetables • ½ cup fresh fruit • ½ medium avocado • ¼ cup fruit purée • 2 tablespoons dried fruit
Full-Fat Dairy	3	• ½ cup milk • ½ cup yogurt or kefir • 1 (1-inch) cube of cheese or 2 tablespoons grated cheese
Proteins	2	• 2 tablespoons ground meat, poultry, or fish or 2 (1-inch) cubes tofu • 2 tablespoons dry beans, peas, or lentils • ½ egg • 1 tablespoon nut butter
Fats	3 to 4	• 1 teaspoon butter, olive oil, or coconut oil

PICKINESS IS NORMAL

A child's first year is a big milestone for many reasons: the first step, the first word, and . . . the first fight over food.

Maybe your baby used to eat almost everything and then—poof—overnight, without any warning, your little one starts refusing previously beloved foods, they become suspicious of certain colors (green is usually the culprit), and they are very vocal about it and totally against trying new foods. Simply put, you find yourself dealing with a toddler.

Don't panic. You didn't do anything wrong and your little one is behaving like many toddlers, if not everyone. Picky eating is a phase in your child's developmental process. Your baby is growing and is slowly understanding that they are someone different from you. They start becoming more independent in different ways, from putting on their own shoes to yelling "I do it, mom!" to deciding what to eat or not eat.

Another thing to remember is that a toddler's growth rate is 30 percent lower than a baby's. That means your 2-year-old actually needs smaller portions and will be less hungry than before.

Sometimes picky eating is related to a temporary physical condition, such as teething or a cold. Our little ones are not fully capable of communicating how they feel. If they are bothered by a growing canine, they might start refusing meals with a simple "I don't like it" when they are in physical discomfort.

It might surprise you, but sometimes emotional battles around food are a reason for picky eating. A tense and stressful approach, bribery, and excessive rewards can all contribute to making food an issue more than a pleasure.

What to do? Keep calm and remind yourself that you are doing a great job as a parent. Raising healthy kids is a long process—it takes time, patience, and a bit of strategy.

Picky eating usually goes away by around 6 years of age. Until then, try to avoid food battles and focus on cooking one meal to enjoy together as a family, which is your first step in turning your picky eater into a happy eater.

TODDLER FEEDING FAQ

Q. How many meals a day should I offer to my toddler?

I would suggest three main meals (breakfast, lunch, and dinner) and two smaller snacks in between but, as always, adjust as needed. Some toddlers like to have a bigger afternoon snack that basically substitutes for dinner and a light snacky dinner later.

Q. My child used to eat more as a baby than as a toddler. Should I worry?

It's completely normal. In their first year, babies go through very rapid growth, sometimes doubling or even tripling their birth weight. After that, growth starts to slow down until they are about 4 years old. Not coinciden-tally, those are the years that children are the "pickiest" about food. So picky eating is not only related to a developmental phase of self-independence, but also to a slower growth rate.

Q. Is there any food I should really avoid offering to my toddler?

According to my pediatrician, the only food to avoid is honey in any form (even cooked) before 12 months. Honey can contain a dangerous bacterium for infants called botulinum that, in the worst-case scenario, can cause an infant's death. By the time they are 1 year old, your baby's digestive system should have developed enough good bacteria that botulinum won't pose a threat.

Foods that might cause choking need to be prepped before being offered to a toddler: Cut grapes in halves or quarters (depending on size), cut blueberries in half, cut meat into very small pieces, make sure carrots are cooked, grind nuts or seeds, and cut raisins in half. Offer sticky foods like nut butters spread on a small piece of bread instead of on a spoon.

The most important thing is to always be around when your little one is eating and keep an eye on them.

Q. Can my toddler eat the same amount of salt and spices that I can eat?

When it comes to little ones, moderation is the key. Spices can help introduce toddlers to a new world of flavors and help broaden their palates. At the same time, a child's taste buds are more sensitive than an adult's and can be easily overstimulated. For little ones, I recommend cutting the spice amount required by a recipe in half. When it comes to salt, I tend to be more strict. A very salty diet is too heavy for your child's kidneys and the amount of sodium naturally present in food is more than enough for a toddler. I would not add any salt for babies younger than 12 months, and salt is used sparingly in the recipes in this book. You can always add a pinch of salt for yourself and the rest of the family when serving the food.

Q. What about allergenic foods?

Food allergies (eggs, dairy, nuts, and shellfish) are very common in children, but recent research suggests that postponing the introduction of allergenic foods doesn't prevent the allergy. That's why the general recommendation is to introduce any food category starting from 6 months of age. Wait until your baby has tolerated a few solid foods before offering an allergenic food. When you are ready to try, follow the three-days-rule: Add a new food and wait three days before adding another one. That's how you will be able to isolate and identify the cause of any allergic reactions.

Of course, if you have any family history of allergies, consult your pediatrician. The good news is that many children outgrow their allergies.

Q. My child cannot stay seated at the table for more than one minute. What do I do?

Toddlers are full of energy, and sitting still in the same place for a long time is often out of their reach. When it comes to eating together, you need to be realistic and expect that your child will stay seated for about 2 minutes per each year of age. For a toddler, that means anything from 5 minutes up to a maximum of 15 minutes in a best-case scenario. You can slowly increase the time you require them to stay at the table, meal by meal. One suggestion is to have your toddler sit at the table only when the food is ready. Don't make the time at the table just about eating. It's important that your child realize that sharing a meal is not just about the food—it's about spending time together. Talk to your toddler, sing together, make jokes, tell stories, and talk about the food.

GETTING YOUR TODDLER TO EAT

As you might have noticed, picky eating cannot be solved with one magic tip (sigh). For me, sharing a meal together as a family has gotten the best results. But there are many other things you can try in addition to eating together to make meals a positive experience for your toddler . . . and for yourself. I usually use some combination of these tips:

Offer something familiar and loved. Sometimes I see a recipe that intrigues me and I adapt it for my kids, but many times I start with foods I know my kids will love and I know I have available in the refrigerator or pantry. One way to reduce picky eating is to always include one or two foods that you know your toddler likes. Worst-case scenario is that your child will eat only those foods, but by offering them alongside less familiar foods, there is a chance your little one will try the new ones. This way, the food isn't a bribe, just part of the meal. The "Eats This? Make That" table on page 12 is designed to help you find recipes based on your kids' favorite foods (or food types). If your toddler is nuts about chicken nuggets, they might be willing to try the Cauliflower and Fish Croquettes (see page 82).

Say, "It's OK if you don't eat it." This is a tough one, I know, but it will be a game-changer for you. Let your child decide how much and which foods to eat within the meal that you prepared. If your toddler only eats a few things or refuses to eat at all, it's OK. I know, it's really difficult to do that; believe me, I've been there. Try to resist the urge to cook something different just for your toddler; that will only encourage your child to be picky because they know they will get a personalized meal. Trust your toddler's appetite. Children need to learn to listen to their bodies so they can self-regulate how much they eat.

Get them hungry! Make sure your kids arrive at the table hungry. That means leaving 2 to 2½ hours between meals and snacks so they have a chance to build up an appetite. If your toddler had a big snack very close to dinnertime, their appetite will be low and you're likely to end up with an untouched plate or many requests for "something different."

Your example makes more impact than any words. Being a model of healthy eating for your kids is very important. If you say "no, thank you" every time you are offered some greens, your toddler will see it as a confirmation that greens are bad.

Get them involved. Being part of a process encourages you to be more involved and committed and that works for toddlers and food, too. Let your little one pick the ingredients from the shelf at the grocery store and place them in the cart, ask her to help you wash the zucchini (water is always attractive to a child), or just place the high chair in the kitchen close to you and give your child some baby spinach leaves to play with while you cook.

Give them a choice. It's not fun to always be told what to do, and your toddler knows that very well. Giving your little one choices between alternatives is a nice compromise and makes them feel "in charge." It can be anything from deciding the recipe to which forks or plates to use.

Make it fun. Your toddler will enjoy the meal if there is a fun component, whether it's shaping the food, inventing a story behind a recipe or an ingredient, using special utensils or dishes, sharing fun daily events, or making jokes.

Eats This? Make That

FOOD FAVE	RECIPE
Avocado	• Green Deviled Eggs (page 33) • Tomato Avocado Sandwich (page 48) • Cucumber, Tomato, Mango, and Avocado Salad (page 69) • Shrimp and Avocado Salad (page 80) • Avocado Yogurt Dip (page 134)
Bread	• Whole-Grain Banana French Toast Sticks (page 45) • Ham and Cheese Calzones (page 51) • Turkey, Tomato, and Pesto Pita Pockets (page 55) • Tuna Panzanella (page 81)
Carrots	• Cream of Carrot and Lentil Soup (page 67) • Quinoa Veggie Croquettes (page 64) • Wintry Beef and Vegetable Stew (page 117) • Carrot Mayo (page 139)
Cheese	• Savory Breakfast Cookies (page 42) • Roasted Broccoli and Ricotta Sandwiches (page 52) • Baked Spinach Pasta Casserole (page 76) • Baked Chicken, Ham, and Mozzarella Rolls (page 107) • Cheesy Beef and Spinach Baked Pasta (page 126)
Chicken Nuggets	• Quinoa Veggie Croquettes (page 64) • Cauliflower and Fish Croquettes (page 82) • Quinoa Chicken Bites (page 103) • Pork and Asparagus Tots with Tomato Salad (page 116)

FOOD FAVE	RECIPE
Chocolate	• Almond Cocoa Butter (page 142) • Orange Quinoa Energy Bites (page 32) • Chocolaty Zucchini Oatmeal (page 38)
Pasta	• Baked Spinach Pasta Casserole (page 76) • Salmon and Broccoli Fusilli (page 83) • Bowties with Chicken and Peas (page 106) • Beef and Zucchini Pasta Bolognese (page 124)
Pizza	• Polenta Pizza Squares (page 58) • Easy Phyllo Pizzas (page 59) • Ham and Cheese Calzones (page 51)
Tomatoes	• Easy Phyllo Pizzas (page 59) • Cucumber, Tomato, Mango, and Avocado Salad (page 69) • Sole and Bulgur–Stuffed Tomatoes (page 88) • Skillet Steak with Tomato and Olives (page 120) • Roasted Tomato Sauce (page 137)
Zucchini	• Spaghetti and Zoodles (page 72) • Shrimp-Stuffed Zucchini Boats (page 87) • Beef and Veggie–Stuffed Zucchini (page 119) • Zucchini Pesto (page 140)

PLANNING AHEAD

Meal planning can make your life easier. Not only does planning ahead help avoid midweek stress when you only have 20 minutes to get dinner on the table before your kid melts down, but it also helps ensure that you're offering a balanced and healthy diet with all the macro- and micro nutrients needed to fuel your kids' growing bodies and minds.

Some people are pros at meal planning. They have the freezer stocked with a month of meals, all labeled and maybe even in color-coded containers. That's great, but unfortunately that's not me—and I'm not the only one who feels that way. In a perfect world, I would love to spend a few hours every Sunday prepping meals for the upcoming week. In real life, it's one of the few days the whole family is off, and we want to spend that time going to the park, biking, attending family events, and simply spending time together. That's why I'm sharing with you my meal planning shortcuts, a more relaxed approach to meal planning that still saves you time and lowers stress during the week when it's time to cook.

Write it down. I do take a few minutes on the weekend to write down a weekly schedule of the main meals I plan to make, so that I don't find myself clueless midweek or tempted to order takeout on Friday. It doesn't need to include every meal. I only write the most important (and potentially stressful) ones, usually dinner. I try to include the kids' favorite recipes, something new I am curious to try, and some easy ones (homemade pizza, pasta) for the tricky nights when we are busier than usual (Fridays or days when kids have sports practice). Once I have the main meals written on a sticky note, it's easier to go to the farmers' market or the grocery store, as I also have the list of the main ingredients I'll need. I'm also flexible with the sequence of meals during the week: It's totally fine to have the chicken pockets on Wednesday instead of Tuesday. The purpose of having a weekly meal plan is to reduce my stress, knowing I have a general plan in place.

Use the same ingredients for multiple meals. Some ingredients are more convenient to buy whole or in large quantities (a head of cauliflower, fish fillets). That's why I use the same ingredient to cook several recipes. A head of cauliflower can be used for fish croquettes on Monday, vegetable Bolognese sauce on Wednesday, soup on Friday, or roasted for a side dish any day of the week.

Involve your kids. Bring your kids with you to the farmers' market or grocery store and have them pick something for that week's dinner. Let them choose one of the recipes in the weekly plan. Being involved means that they will be more likely to try what "they" made.

Double up on freezer-friendly favorites. When preparing a recipe, double the ingredients and freeze the extra quantity for a future crazy busy night. I always do this for meatballs, lasagna, and pasta sauces.

COOKING TOGETHER

Cooking with kids is fun. Yes, it will be messy. Yes, it takes more time. Still, it's more fun and creates precious family memories and a positive attitude toward food.

The recipes I share in this book are meant to be prepared by you, but that doesn't mean you can't have a little help here and there from your toddler. It will make them feel included, the final recipe will magically become "their" recipe, and the chances of it being eaten will go way up. Here are a few suggestions for ways your child can help:

Let your little one add ingredients to the bowl. When baking a cake, measure out the ingredients in separate bowls and let your toddler pour them in while you mix.

Let them add the finishing touch. They can sprinkle oregano on a pizza or tear basil leaves and sprinkle them into a bowl of pasta.

Let them press buttons. Toddlers love this. My little one is still thrilled to push the "on" button of the food processor and practically gets hypnotized when watching smoothies purée in the blender.

Let them play with the pizza dough. Give your little one a small ball of pizza dough to play while you prepare the family pizza. Have them help you put on the pizza toppings. You might end up with a concentration of ingredients in one spot, but that's an easy fix.

Let them wash the veggies. I don't know any kid who doesn't love to play with water. I used a toddler kitchen step so my kids could safely reach the sink. I'd put the vegetables in a bowl, then they would fill it with water and wash them. It was one of their favorite things to do.

Although I love cooking with my kids, I do have a list of things they know they are not allowed to do at all or without my supervision. Touching anything on the stovetop when the flame is on, being around the stove when mom is cooking, touching any raw meat or fish, or using knives or scissors without mom's supervision. (I would not suggest that a 2-year-old use a knife, but a 4-year-old kid can start handling scissors or practicing with a plastic kid's knife under your supervision.)

FOOD FUN, NOT FIGHTS

You may have heard that you should avoid saying the word "no" and try to find softer ways to discourage your toddler from doing something. Rather than saying something like "No, don't rip the leaf from the plant," say something like "Let's be gentle with this plant. Its leaves need to grow strong like you do."

The concept is to switch a negative situation into something more positive that helps your toddler develop autonomy and initiative. This idea works with food and eating, too.

Fighting with your toddler over food and using tactics like "You can have dessert if you eat your veggies" or pleading "Just three more bites" can lead to even more tense and stressful attitudes toward food and mealtime. Let's do the opposite and add some fun and brightness! Here are some ideas for making mealtimes fun:

Make the plate look fun. Kids eat with their eyes first, and arranging the food in a creative way can make a difference. Cut the food into fun shapes, like transforming a strawberry into a heart or using cookie cutters (my best friend in the toddler kitchen!). Place sweet peas on top of a frittata in the shape of a star or transform a pancake into a smiley face with just one strawberry and two blueberries. You don't need elaborate bento box–style skills—you can create something kids will like in a few steps and little time.

Create a story around a recipe. If the fun plate is not your thing, make up a story about the food you are serving (I had a fun one about "Grandma Tina Tagliatelle" that my kids still enjoy) or around an ingredient ("The Broccoli Woods Adventure").

Get educational. Ask your kids to count the peas on their plate. Tell them to eat one and then count them again. How many are left?

Create a sensory food game. It's totally normal for kids to want to play with and explore their food. They are much more likely to try new foods if you encourage them to get familiar with them. Try asking your kids to create a tower with cucumber slices. How many can they stack before it falls? If they eat one slice, will the tower hold?

Show them the power of food. I'm very into the nutritional value of food and I like to share that knowledge with my kids by equating different types of food with superheroes. I tell my kids that every ingredient has a superpower, and if they try it, they will have that superpower, too. Carrots and orange bell peppers will make them see far, far away. Blueberries will help them think faster. Salmon will make their brains stronger. Greens will make their bodies stronger. (Why else is the Hulk green?) When they get older, you can move from a superhero approach to a more scientific, but still kid-friendly one. For example, blueberries have something called "antioxidants" in them, which are like defense soldiers that protect healthy cells.

PITFALLS TO AVOID

I just wrote that food fights, bribes, and pleading do not work in the long run and cause tons of stress in the family. Still, I resorted to all three tactics with my kids at least a few times. Does that make me a bad parent? I don't think so. As parents, we want to encourage our kids to become healthy eaters, and being imperfectly human, sometimes we choose short-term solutions. It's OK. But for long-term results, here are some short-term fixes to avoid:

Hiding the Vegetables

To hide or not to hide the vegetables? That's a great question. It's so easy to add a few spinach leaves to a banana smoothie. Your toddler will not guess you added them, nor taste them, and they will get the lovely nutrients. Short-term result: Your toddler is eating spinach. Long-term result: Your toddler will still not like spinach and will be unlikely to voluntarily eat it on their own. My solution? I recommend a "conscious hiding" approach. I would prepare the smoothie with my little one, adding all the ingredients, spinach included, and talk about all the ingredients to make him aware. Later, I would cook a kid-friendly spinach side dish and remind him that if the spinach in the smoothie tasted good, this one will taste good, too.

Threats, Pleading, and Bribes

"If you eat two more bites of fish, you can have a candy." Short-term result: Your toddler will eat the salmon and the candy. Long-term result: In your toddler's mind, the candy is the precious reward for eating the yucky salmon. Your child may have eaten the salmon, but you might need a visit to the dentist after eating all that candy. Reducing the pressure on food and mealtimes is the key.

The "Division of Responsibility" approach, developed by Ellyn Satter, a registered dietitian and authority on feeding children, is my favorite approach because it ends food fights, relieves the stress, and (most importantly) it works. A parent is responsible for what, when, and where the toddler eats, while the toddler is responsible for whether they will eat and how much. If you can be at peace with the idea that your little one might eat only a few bites of their meal and only of the food that they like, you have already won in the long-term. Eventually your child will eat what's in front of them and start discovering new foods to like.

ANYTIME FOOD FUN

To create a positive approach to food, there are many food-themed activities that you can enjoy with your toddler outside mealtimes.

- Food art time is one of my favorites: Painting with veggies is so much fun. Celery sticks can be incredible brushes, and you can use a cookie cutter or a knife to transform a carrot or a potato into a stamp. You can also place vegetables or fruit on paper, trace their shape, then remove them and play the "What vegetable is this?" game.

- Pretend cooking in the backyard or at the beach is a fun game, too. Did you ever make a mud pie or a sand pizza using shells and pebbles as toppings?

- Whenever possible, I take my kids on a tour of a vegetable garden or a fruit farm. We can see how veggies or fruit grow, look for insects or little animals, and taste sun-ripened produce. It's a lovely experience.

- As technology is part of our kids' lives, I've also found interesting food-related apps to entertain them. Search "educational food toddler games" and you will find the latest ones.

- Music also plays an essential role in your toddler's development. You'd be surprised to discover how many food-related toddler songs are available. Our favorite one is "Vegetarian Zombie."

YOUR TODDLER-FRIENDLY KITCHEN

When I come back from a summer trip, it's my chance to clean up the refrigerator, pantry, and freezer and also check that I have the healthy staples on hand for my recipes. My checklist looks a little like this:

Pantry

Coconut oil. Choose organic virgin coconut oil. Coconut oil is very sensitive to heat, so depending on how cold it is outside, you may open your coconut oil and find it in liquid form or it may be white and solid. Don't worry: It's fine and good in both forms.

Dried fruit. I like to use raisins, apricots, and dates as natural sweeteners for desserts.

Dried herbs and spices. Some of my favorite seasonings to add extra flavor to dishes are oregano, thyme, marjoram, paprika, cumin, coriander, turmeric, and garlic powder.

Flours and meals. Whole-wheat, rice, tapioca, flaxseed meal, and almond meal are my top choices. Even if my kids do not have a specific allergy, I like their diet to be as diversified as possible. Whole-wheat is my go-to flour for baking, but if I want a gluten-free option, I use rice flour or tapioca flour. Flaxseed meal helps when I want a substitute for eggs in a recipe and almond meal is my favorite alternative to breadcrumbs, both as a gluten-free option and to add more nutrients to the recipe.

Garlic. I'm Italian—fresh garlic is a must-have.

Nut butters. My kids love almond butter, but feel free to use any other nut butter you like.

Nuts and seeds. I like to keep a variety of nuts and seeds on hand, including almonds, pecans, pine nuts, chia seeds, and hemp seeds (keep them refrigerated once opened) because I like to offer variety to the kids so they will not get bored eating the same almonds day after day. And, when nuts play a big role in a recipe, like in the Almond Cocoa Butter (page 142), changing the nut variety can change the flavor in a new and interesting way.

Olive oil. I like to keep both extra-virgin olive oil and coconut oil on hand for cooking and baking. I'm picky about my olive oil; it needs to be high quality because I use it at room temperature in many recipes and you can really taste the difference. Store olive oils in a dark place or in a dark glass bottle. They don't like direct sun—the flavor will change and not for the better.

Pasta. This is one of the most toddler-friendly ingredients you can get. I like to have a variety of shapes and types on hand: traditional durum wheat, organic, and not enriched, all in different shapes and sizes. For the smallest kids, I try to find the smallest shapes. Fusilli, penne, elbows, and shells are my favorites. I also keep a few packages of gluten-free pasta on hand to balance our diet. Varieties made with red lentils, chickpeas, rice, and corn flour are improving and keep their shape better when cooked.

Rice. I prefer brown rice for side dishes, plus a few special varieties—like black Venus rice for rice salads and Arborio or Carnaroli for risotto (which has more starch and keeps its texture once cooked, which makes a super creamy risotto).

Sweeteners. I prefer to use less-processed sweeteners like local honey (remember not to offer honey to babies younger than 12 months), maple syrup, and coconut sugar in my baked goods, for sweetening yogurt, and for drizzling over pancakes and waffles.

Unsweetened cocoa. This is a great ingredient to turn something healthy like oatmeal or a smoothie into a chocolaty "treat"—all kids love chocolate, right?

Vinegars. Balsamic vinegar and apple cider vinegar are great to keep on hand for making a quick dressing or dip and for adding seasoning to your dishes.

Whole grains. Some of my favorites include couscous, bulgur, quinoa, and farro. These are mild-flavored, fiber-rich alternatives to pasta and rice, and I use them when I want to switch up ingredients but still keep it familiar for my kids.

Refrigerator

Eggs. The best eggs are organic, cage-free, and pasture-raised.

Greek yogurt. Plain yogurt is what I keep on hand, and I can sweeten it naturally with a drizzle of honey or maple syrup if I want. I can also use it for savory recipes. Greek yogurt is thicker than regular yogurt and kids seem to like the texture better.

Kefir. I often add one teaspoon of plain kefir to the yogurt I give to the kids for some extra natural probiotics.

Milk. I use organic, lactose-free whole milk. I'm lactose-intolerant, and it's easier for me to have one container of milk in the refrigerator instead of two.

Parmesan cheese. I could write a whole book about Parmesan cheese. Being aged, it has a low lactose content, which makes it easier to digest for kids. It's loaded with flavor, so it really makes a difference in any recipe. I prefer my Parmesan to be aged for 24 months. I also grate it as soon as I buy it to save time later.

Freezer

Berries. Fresh berries are great, but I think frozen ones are perfect to use in smoothies or to bake with. I tend to keep frozen berries or other fruit that is either not in season or difficult to find locally, such as pineapple, mango, or açai.

Chicken breast. I like to use certified organic and pasture-raised chicken. It makes a big difference in terms of chemicals you really don't want in your body. I also prefer skinless and boneless for cooking ease and versatility.

Edamame. Unsalted, still in the pods. I simply take a handful from the freezer, put them in a microwave-safe bowl, and add a pinch of sea salt. Cover with a damp paper towel and microwave for one minute. The fun is not only in eating them but also in squishing them out of the pod.

Ground beef. Certified organic and grass-fed.

Peas. I prefer organic sweet peas. They are great as an ice pack if the kids get hurt, too.

Salmon fillets. I try to buy wild-caught as opposed to farm-raised salmon, which often has added artificial colors.

Shrimp. To keep things simple, I usually buy frozen shrimp that are shelled with the heads removed. Keep small shrimp on hand for toddlers and larger ones for adults. The smaller they are, the quicker they will cook. But you can always cut larger shrimp into small pieces for little hands to enjoy.

White fish fillets. I love buying fresh fish from my fishmonger, but I also like to have a selection of white fish fillets such as mahi-mahi, Dover sole, tilapia, halibut, or catfish waiting in the freezer. As with salmon, I buy wild-caught fish whenever possible, not farm-raised. If farm-raised is all that is available, I check the ingredients for information about the conditions the fish are farmed under and if any artificial coloring has been added.

CHOOSING QUALITY INGREDIENTS

I grew up in a small town in Northern Italy, and at that time there was no need to label produce "organic" or to check if a food contained hormones or antibiotics. Fruits and vegetables were farmed naturally, and no one used antibiotics or hormones on their animals. But farming practices have changed, and today it is essential to be informed about where our food comes from and its quality.

I'm the kind of customer who reads labels and checks all the ingredients on the package before buying anything. At the same time, I'm also a mom with a family budget to keep under control. For fresh produce, I try to buy local and organic as much as possible. Every year I check the Dirty Dozen—a list of fruits and vegetables known to have high pesticide residuals. If the produce I want is on the list, I buy only organic. To see the current list, search for "dirty dozen" and the current year. For produce not on the list, it's less important to buy organic, but I buy organic if the price is reasonable.

For meat, I buy only certified organic, as it's the only way to be sure that there are no hormones or antibiotics. It's expensive, but I do not compromise on meat—I'd rather use less to save money. For seafood, I check for two things: Is it farmed or wild? And does it have added colors? Wild-caught fish is best and that's what I buy when I can find it. When it comes to salmon, producers often add color to give the fish a brighter color. Color is not an indicator of quality, so I avoid anything with artificially added colors, including foods such as cereals, cookies, or chips. There are so many ways to naturally color food without using chemicals.

Other labels to look for when buying food are grass-fed, pasture-raised, locally produced, and cage-free (for eggs). They are nice extras, and I buy ingredients with these labels when the budget allows.

EQUIPMENT YOU WILL NEED

You might be surprised to know that you probably already have all the basic equipment you need to cook the recipes in this book. These are the essentials to have in the kitchen:

To Prep and Cook

Cutting board. I like large, sturdy wooden cutting boards, and I also have a very thin plastic one that I place on top of the wooden one when I work with raw meat or fish.

Food processor or high-speed blender. It's best to have one that is powerful and has multi-blades. I trust my Ninja. If it can properly blend almond butter, it should be good for the other recipes in this book.

Glass storage containers with lids. I decided to go plastic-free a few years ago and I will never regret it. Keep a few containers in different sizes that are microwave-safe and freezer-safe.

Immersion blender. When you have a baby or toddler in the house, an immersion blender is a must. Look for a metal blade, a strong engine, and one that's easy to clean.

Knives. You don't need tons of knives, just three sharp ones—small, medium, and large.

Muffin pans (regular, mini, maxi). Pans with six wells are perfect for creating a "tasting" meal or snack for your little ones.

Skillet. Make sure you have two—one large and one medium. I'm in love with the Titanium Bialetti line.

Stainless steel pots. Make sure you have one large, one medium, and one small stainless steel pot.

Steamer. The stainless steel pot attachment to place on top is fine, but I find adjustable silicone removable steamers easier to use and to store.

Vegetable peeler. I have an ingenious peeler that looks like a portable pencil sharpener and I love it. But use whatever works for you.

To Make It Easy and Fun

Cookie cutters. Have the basic shapes for sure (hearts, stars, circles), but there is no limit to what you can add to your collection (holiday-themed, numbers, letters, seasons).

Instant Pot®. Although it does take up space on the countertop, the Instant Pot® will save you tons of time when making meals.

Kids' kitchen step. A sturdy and safe step helps your little one reach the countertop and sink and really get involved.

Kids' plates. Sometimes, instead of a fancy food presentation, a colorful or divided plate has the same effect. Bobo&Boo, Oogaa, iPlay Baby, Bamboo Bamboo, Baby Eatery, and Ezpz all make great choices.

Kids' utensils. There are so many fun and eco-friendly choices for kid-friendly forks, spoons, knives, and learning chopsticks.

Ice pop molds. Silicone molds come in many fun shapes for both little hands and big hands.

Salad spinner. I cannot count the number of times I've let my kids play with the salad spinner to dry out basil leaves or spinach while I was cooking.

Spiralizer. To easily transform zucchini, carrots, and squash into spaghetti zoodles, this is the tool to have. I have a compact, portable one that is inexpensive and doesn't take up a lot of space, but any spiralizer will work.

Straws. Keep colorful silicone or stainless steel straws on hand to make drinking smoothies even more fun. Bamboo straws are a new lovely find and they are fun, too. Any reusable straw will work; just try to avoid plastic.

Waffle maker. Kids love waffles and you can also use a waffle maker to cook grilled cheese sandwiches.

ABOUT THE RECIPES

Are you ready to start cooking? I assure you, it will be easy and take less effort than you might expect. You will be able to serve yummy and healthy meals and snacks to your toddler and the entire family—and sit with them to enjoy the meal yourself. How great is that?

The recipes are divided into Not-Just-Muffins Breakfast, Handhelds for Little Hands, Vegetables Your Kids Will (Might) Eat, Fish Stick–Free Seafood Meals, Non-Nugget Chicken Dinners, and Beyond the Meatball Meaty Mains. There is even a chapter called Just Add This with dips, sauces, and spreads that your kids will love (and that you'll be able to use to make a meal more appealing to your little one). I focused on main meals, as I consider them the trickiest to get toddlers to eat (all toddlers will eat snacks, right?). And if you are looking for snack ideas, many of the recipes can be made in snack sizes or made portable for on-the-go meals and lunch boxes.

Many of the recipes have an optional To make it more toddler-friendly step that will help you easily "toddlerize" the recipe for your child—whether that's by transforming the food itself or changing up the presentation to make it more appealing or safer for toddlers to eat.

Every recipe is marked with labels—including Dairy-free, Egg-free, Gluten-free, Nut-free, Vegan, and Vegetarian—so you can easily find recipes that will work for your family's dietary needs.

All of these recipes are easy, but there are also labels that indicate specifically *how* they are easy, including:

30 Minutes or Less, which gets the recipe on the table in half an hour.

5 Ingredients or Less, which indicates that the recipe uses 5 main ingredients or less, not including oil, water, salt, or pepper.

One-Pot, meaning that the dish is cooked in one vessel, so you'll have less clean up later.

Freezer-friendly, meaning that the dish freezes well, which will help you make sure that you always have something ready to cook, even on really busy nights.

Most recipes also have a tip, including:

Make it fun. Whether it's by switching up the food presentation, engaging your toddler in making the meal, or sharing a fun game or story inspired by the recipe, these tips are all about increasing the fun for your child.

Prep help. A shortcut or easy hack that will save you prep time and cooking time.

Swap it! A tip that will offer alternatives for ingredients to make a recipe allergen-free, vegetarian, vegan, or simply to give you a more toddler-friendly option.

If all else fails . . . Every recipe in this book has been toddler-tested, but all toddlers are different and sometimes you just need something a little extra to coax your kiddo to try the food. I've been there many times. Here I've offered more ways to further "toddlerize" a recipe—a kid-friendly ingredient to add, a different way to present a food, or an ingredient to skip.

KEEP CALM AND TRY, TRY AGAIN

Easy and simple are the key words for this book. Even though I'm super passionate about cooking, I sometimes still find myself stuck with only 30 minutes to prepare a healthy and inviting meal for the family, with the kids complaining that they will starve to death if they are not fed in 30 seconds. Cooking every day for a family with little kids can be challenging and picky eating makes it even harder. Having a set of kid-friendly recipes on hand that are healthy, tasty, and appropriate for the whole family can be useful and lower the pressure at mealtimes.

I hope this cookbook gives you ideas, tips, and inspiration for new recipes and family meals, but more than that, I hope to share with you a positive and optimistic attitude toward family mealtimes. I want to reassure you that it's OK if your toddler doesn't eat everything you serve or refuses to try new foods, and that it's totally fine if you end up serving take-out pizza one night—none of this makes you a bad parent. No one is perfect; just keep trying and don't give up! Picky eating is a phase and this, too, shall pass. Just remember to put less pressure on food and eating, continue to expose your kids to healthy options, and, most importantly, eat the same meal together as often as you can. You'll find that, over time, your little ones will develop a taste for simple and nutritious food.

Pink Almond Waffles, page 40

2

NOT-JUST-MUFFINS BREAKFAST

I wish every breakfast could be Saturday morning. No school, no work, no rush—just the relaxed pleasure of eating together and planning the weekend. During the week, there are so many things to get done in a small amount of time, which makes preparing a balanced breakfast for a growing toddler a challenge, especially one that will also please the rest of the family. Here are my favorite breakfast ideas that will hopefully make your crazy mornings a whole lot easier. From sweet to savory, very textured to super smooth, each recipe has been tried, tested, and approved by toddlers and adults and they will offer your family a great start to *any* day!

Orange Quinoa Energy Bites 32

Green Deviled Eggs 33

Very Berry Grape Smoothies 34

Peanut Butter and Banana
  Smoothies 35

Immune-Boosting Smoothies 37

Chocolaty Zucchini Oatmeal 38

Mixed-Berry Chia Pudding 39

Pink Almond Waffles 40

Green Pancakes with
  Blueberries 41

Savory Breakfast Cookies 42

Super Green Frittata Bread 43

Blueberry Yogurt Cake 44

Whole-Grain Banana French Toast
  Sticks 45

ORANGE QUINOA ENERGY BITES

Serves 6 | **Prep time:** 15 minutes

DAIRY-FREE, EGG-FREE, GLUTEN-FREE, VEGAN, 30 MINUTES OR LESS

The combination of chocolate and orange is one of the most delicious pairings ever. In the process of developing a yummy baby treat without any additional sugar and loaded with healthy nutrients, I ended up with an addictive treat for parents, too. I like to use black quinoa because it's sweeter than other varieties, but any color will work. I recommend using sulfur-free apricots, if possible. Sulfur dioxide is a preservative used to prevent dried fruit from spoiling and to retain its bright color. In small amounts, it's classified safe, but in very sensitive people, it can lead to breathing problems, skin rashes, and tummy ache. As I'm cooking for kids, I prefer not to take that risk.

½ cup roasted almonds

¼ cup sulfur-free dried apricots

5 Medjool dates, pitted

1 cup unsweetened coconut flakes, divided

1 cup cooked black quinoa

¼ cup unsweetened cocoa powder

3 tablespoons almond butter

1 tablespoon ground flaxseed

1 orange, zested and juiced

1. Process or blend the almonds, apricots, dates, and ½ cup coconut flakes in a food processor or high-speed blender until smooth. Add the quinoa, cocoa powder, almond butter, ground flaxseed, and orange zest and juice and process or blend until smooth.

2. Pour the remaining ½ cup coconut flakes into a small bowl. Using your hands, roll 1 teaspoon of the quinoa-fruit mixture into a ball and roll it in the coconut flakes. Place the ball on a large plate.

3. Repeat with the rest of the mixture.

4. To make it more toddler-friendly: For kids who don't like too much texture, omit the coconut coating on some of the balls.

5. Store the balls in an airtight container in the refrigerator for up to 2 weeks, or freeze them for up to 3 months.

Swap it! Nut allergies are very common, so if you are looking for a nut-free version, use roasted sunflower seeds instead of the almonds and sunflower butter instead of the almond butter. The bites will be less nutty, of course, but still yummy.

GREEN DEVILED EGGS

Serves 4 | **Prep time:** 10 minutes / **Cook time:** 12 minutes

DAIRY-FREE, GLUTEN-FREE, NUT-FREE, VEGETARIAN, 30 MINUTES OR LESS, 5 INGREDIENTS OR LESS

Cooking a recipe inspired by a favorite family book makes meals easier and fun, as your toddler already has a positive connection with the story. We loved reading *Green Eggs and Ham* together at the dinner table while enjoying these green eggs. The recipe is a healthy toddler version of traditional deviled eggs: good healthy fats and nothing spicy. For a fun presentation, transform your eggs into super cute chicks by using a tiny piece of carrot for a beak and black olives for eyes.

4 medium eggs

1 Hass avocado, peeled
  and pitted

2 teaspoons lemon juice

¼ teaspoon sweet paprika

Pinch sea salt

1. Place the eggs in a saucepan filled with cold water and bring to a boil over medium-high heat. Lower the heat to medium-low and simmer for 12 minutes. Drain the water and let the eggs cool until you can remove the shells with your hands.

2. Cut the eggs in half, remove the yolks, and put them in a bowl. Set the egg whites on a serving plate.

3. Add the avocado, lemon juice, sweet paprika, and salt to the egg yolks and mix together into a smooth cream with a fork.

4. Using a spoon, fill the egg whites with the egg yolk mixture. Alternatively, you can transfer the yolk mixture to a piping bag and pipe it into the egg whites.

5. Serve immediately or store the eggs in an airtight container in the refrigerator for up to 2 days.

If all else fails . . . For an even more toddler-friendly egg yolk mixture, add 1 tablespoon mayonnaise.

VERY BERRY GRAPE SMOOTHIES

Serves 4 | **Prep time:** 15 minutes

EGG-FREE, GLUTEN-FREE, NUT-FREE, VEGETARIAN, 30 MINUTES OR LESS

I love to add veggies to our smoothies. It's a nice way to get your toddler accustomed to them, starting from the first meal of the day, and the veggies in this recipe totally blend in with the other flavors. The riced cauliflower in this smoothie will not only provide fiber and antioxidants but also a creamy texture. You can add half a banana, which will make the smoothie even creamier. For more natural sweetness, use green grapes instead of black.

¾ cup blueberries

¾ cup blackberries

¾ cup frozen riced
 cauliflower

½ cup coconut water

½ cup seedless
 black grapes

3 tablespoons plain yogurt
 or plain kefir

1 tablespoon ground
 flaxseed

1 tablespoon honey
 (optional, if grapes are
 not sweet enough)

1. Put the blueberries, blackberries, cauliflower, coconut water, grapes, yogurt, ground flaxseed, and honey (if using) in a food processor or high-speed blender and process or blend for 1 minute, until smooth.

2. The smoothie can be stored in an airtight container in the refrigerator for up to 4 hours.

Make it fun. To get my kids involved and passionate about smoothies, I invented the "Guess the ingredient" game. I tell the kids that their smoothies have some secret ingredients. They cannot see or peek. They usually start to giggle as I prepare the smoothie and keep telling them, "Don't look! I saw you, turn around!" Then we have fun together tasting the smoothie and guessing which ingredients I used. I give them clues like, "This ingredient makes you see in the dark (carrots)."

PEANUT BUTTER AND BANANA SMOOTHIES

Serves 2 | **Prep time:** 15 minutes

EGG-FREE, GLUTEN-FREE, VEGETARIAN, 30 MINUTES OR LESS

Here is the perfect smoothie for kids who need to gain weight or who don't like a regular breakfast in the morning. It tastes like vanilla–peanut butter ice cream, super smooth and creamy. Loaded with nutrients, it's a big hit with little ones and adults. Toddlers love to push buttons. Let your child start the food processor and quickly get hypnotized by the ingredients turning around and around in a fun vortex. Serve with a jumbo silicone straw and have fun!

1 ripe banana, cut in pieces

¾ cup whole milk

½ cup old-fashioned oats

3 tablespoons plain
Greek yogurt

2 tablespoons
peanut butter

1 tablespoon ground
flaxseed

1 tablespoon maple syrup
(optional)

1 teaspoon vanilla extract

½ teaspoon ground
cinnamon

1. Place the banana, milk, oats, yogurt, peanut butter, ground flaxseed, maple syrup (if using), vanilla, and cinnamon in a food processor or high-speed blender and process or blend for 1 minute, until smooth.

2. The smoothie can be stored in an airtight container in the refrigerator for up to 4 hours.

Swap it! To make this dairy-free, simply use almond milk instead of whole milk and coconut yogurt instead of Greek yogurt. I have also used coconut cream, which gives the smoothie a lovely coconutty taste.

IMMUNE-BOOSTING SMOOTHIES

Serves 2 | Prep time: 15 minutes
DAIRY FREE, EGG-FREE, GLUTEN-FREE, NUT-FREE, VEGETARIAN, 30 MINUTES OR LESS

This refreshing smoothie is loaded with immune-boosting ingredients, from anti-inflammatory ginger and turmeric to antibacterial honey and pineapple, a natural cough suppressant. You can see why I'm a big fan: Smoothies are an easy way to offer your toddler a powerful combo of nutrients in just one sip. They can be prepared in no time in the morning and poured into a travel cup to drink on the way to school. To make things even easier, much of the fruit can be added frozen so you will save time peeling and chopping in the morning.

1 cup chopped pineapple

1 small ripe banana, cut in pieces

½ pear, peeled, cored, and cut in pieces

½ mango, peeled, pitted, and cut in pieces

¼ cup coconut water

1 tablespoon honey

1 teaspoon hemp seeds

½ teaspoon grated fresh turmeric or ¼ teaspoon ground turmeric

¼ teaspoon grated fresh ginger or ⅛ teaspoon ground ginger

2 kale leaves, tough stems removed

1. Put the pineapple, banana, pear, mango, coconut water, honey, hemp seeds, turmeric, ginger, and kale in a food processor or high-speed blender and process or blend for 1 minute, until smooth.

2. The smoothie can be stored in an airtight container in the refrigerator for up to 4 hours.

Make it fun. Fill toddler-friendly ice pop molds with the smoothie mix, freeze them, and get ready for a fun frozen-fruit picnic in the backyard.

CHOCOLATY ZUCCHINI OATMEAL

Serves 2 | **Prep time:** 10 minutes / **Cook time:** 5 minutes
DAIRY-FREE, EGG-FREE, GLUTEN-FREE, NUT-FREE, VEGAN, 30 MINUTES OR LESS

Nothing beats warm oatmeal in the morning. Whether you're 18 months or 80 years old, warm oatmeal is always comforting and homey. This lovely version has a chocolaty flavor (super toddler-friendly) and grated zucchini for more nutrients (super parent-friendly). You can use fresh fruit to make funny faces on top.

1 small zucchini

1 cup coconut milk

Pinch sea salt

½ cup old-fashioned oats

1 tablespoon unsweetened cocoa powder

1 ripe banana, mashed

1 teaspoon chia seeds

1 teaspoon ground flaxseed

Seasonal fruit, for topping (optional)

1. Finely grate the zucchini into a bowl, retaining any extra liquid. Set aside.

2. In a saucepan over medium-high heat, mix together the coconut milk and salt and bring to a boil. Lower the heat to medium, add the oats and zucchini, and cook for 1 minute. Remove from the heat, cover, and let stand for 4 minutes.

3. Add the cocoa powder, mashed banana, chia seeds, and ground flaxseed and mix well. Serve warm, topped with fruit (if using).

4. **To make it more toddler-friendly:** Use the fruit to make a funny face on top of the oatmeal or give your little ones some cut-up fruit to make their own.

Swap it! Your toddler doesn't like green food? Swap the green zucchini for yellow squash. The finished dish will have a reassuring and comforting yellowish color.

MIXED-BERRY CHIA PUDDING

Serves 2 | **Prep time:** 5 minutes, plus at least 2 hours to chill

DAIRY-FREE, EGG-FREE, GLUTEN-FREE, NUT-FREE, VEGETARIAN, 5 INGREDIENTS OR LESS

When breakfast looks and tastes like dessert, the morning can only be a sunny one. This chia pudding is an easy recipe and one you can prepare the night before. In addition, chia seeds are an excellent source of omega-3 fatty acids and are easier to digest than flaxseed. If you don't have time to eat in the morning, spoon the pudding into a container with a lid, like a small mason jar, and eat it on the go.

1 cup coconut milk

4 tablespoons chia seeds

2 tablespoons mixed-berry jam or Apricot Chia Jam (see page 143)

1 tablespoon vanilla extract

2 teaspoons honey

Sliced almonds and fruit, for topping (optional)

1. In a bowl, mix together the coconut milk, chia seeds, jam, vanilla, honey, and sliced almonds and fruit (if using).

2. Let sit for 2 to 3 minutes. Stir the mixture again until there are no lumps.

3. Divide the mixture into 2 containers, cover, and refrigerate for at least 2 hours or overnight.

4. To make it more toddler-friendly: Use an immersion blender to purée the mixture into a completely smooth and creamy pudding.

5. To serve, remove the pudding from the refrigerator and let sit on the counter for a few minutes. Top with almonds and your toddler's favorite fruit.

Swap it! This recipe is easy to personalize to your toddler's taste. You can change the milk (regular, coconut, almond, goat) and the jam (berries, apricots, peaches, figs); for those under 1 year old, use maple syrup instead of honey.

PINK ALMOND WAFFLES

Serves 4 | **Prep time:** 10 minutes / **Cook time:** 10 minutes
GLUTEN-FREE, VEGETARIAN, 30 MINUTES OR LESS

Add a touch of pink to your waffles and transform them into "unicorn superfood"! The almond meal provides an extra boost of protein to start the day with the right energy. This is a great recipe to let your little one press the buttons on the food processor and have fun looking at how the different ingredients combine into a pretty pink batter. Natural ingredients change color with heat: Your pink batter will turn into brownish–pale pink waffles. Don't let your little one be scared by the change of color—make it a fun learning moment by asking them to guess what the final color will be!

2 medium eggs

1 cup almond meal

½ cup plain yogurt

1 ripe banana

3 tablespoons maple syrup, plus more for serving

3 tablespoons coconut oil

½ small cooked beet, chopped

1 teaspoon baking powder

½ teaspoon baking soda

¼ teaspoon sea salt

1. Preheat a waffle maker according to the manufacturer's instructions.

2. Put the eggs, almond meal, yogurt, banana, maple syrup, coconut oil, beet, baking powder, baking soda, and salt into a food processor and process until smooth.

3. Pour 3 to 4 tablespoons of the mixture onto the waffle maker and cook according to the manufacturer's instructions. Repeat with the rest of the batter. Place each waffle in a single layer on a wire rack until ready to serve. If you stack them, they will get soggy.

4. Serve the waffles warm with maple syrup and fresh fruit.

5. To make it more toddler-friendly: Serve with chocolate-hazelnut spread.

Prep help: Don't have a waffle maker? No worries, make pancakes instead. The batter is exactly the same and you will only need a small sauté pan or skillet and a spatula to flip the pancakes.

GREEN PANCAKES WITH BLUEBERRIES

Serves 4 | **Prep time:** 10 minutes / **Cook time:** 10 minutes
NUT-FREE, VEGETARIAN, 30 MINUTES OR LESS

Pancakes are our favorite breakfast on Sunday mornings. The kids love decorating them, using chocolate-hazelnut spread to glue pieces of fruit on top. I like to enrich the batter by adding unusual nutritious ingredients like baby spinach. To coordinate with the green color, I top the pancakes with blueberries. To optimize time in the morning, I prepare the pancake batter in the evening and refrigerate it overnight. The next day, I simply whisk the batter to get it fluffy again and pour it on the griddle.

¾ cup whole-wheat flour

1 tablespoon potato starch or tapioca starch

½ teaspoon baking soda

1 teaspoon baking powder

Pinch sea salt

1 cup packed fresh baby spinach

1 medium egg

2 tablespoons coconut oil, plus 1 tablespoon for frying

¾ cup whole milk

¼ cup maple syrup, for serving (optional)

1 cup fresh blueberries (cut in half, if very large), for serving

1. Combine the flour, potato starch, baking soda, baking powder, salt, spinach, egg, coconut oil, and milk in a food processor and process until smooth.

2. In a large sauté pan or skillet over medium heat, warm 1 tablespoon coconut oil. Pour 1 tablespoon of the batter into the center of the pan and gently shake the pan to give the batter a nice round shape.

3. Cook the pancake for 3 minutes, until bubbles appear. Flip and continue cooking for an additional 2 minutes, until browned. Transfer to a large plate. Repeat with the remaining batter, stacking the pancakes one on top of the other to keep them warm and fluffy. You should be able to make 10 to 12 pancakes.

4. Serve warm with a drizzle of maple syrup (if using) and a handful of blueberries.

5. *To make it more toddler-friendly:* Cut large blueberries in half and use them to make a smiley face on top.

Make it fun. Make sushi pancakes! Spread 1 teaspoon cream cheese on top of a pancake. Line 4 or 5 blueberries in a row in the center of the pancake and roll it up. Cut the pancake crosswise like a sushi roll.

SAVORY BREAKFAST COOKIES

Serves 4 | **Prep time:** 15 minutes / **Cook time:** 15 minutes
NUT-FREE, 30 MINUTES OR LESS

Savory cookies? Yes! Your toddler will be happily surprised by the cheesy and salty flavors of these yummy breakfast cookies, which can do double-duty as an afternoon snack or as an addition to a lunch box. Your child can pick the cookie-cutter shape to use and help cut out the cookies. They might not be perfect, but they will be made with love. For the many families that need to rush out of house in the morning, these cookies can be eaten in the car as an on-the-go breakfast without leaving a mess.

¾ cup whole-grain flour

½ cup ground flaxseed

10 tablespoons cold
   butter, diced

1 cup grated
   Parmesan cheese

3½ ounces cooked ham,
   shredded

1 medium egg

Pinch sea salt, plus more
   for topping

1 medium egg yolk

Flaxseed, for topping

1. In a stand mixer on medium, mix together the flour, ground flaxseed, butter, Parmesan cheese, ham, egg, and salt for 2 to 3 minutes, until it forms a compact dough.

2. Preheat the oven to 400°F. Line a baking sheet with parchment paper.

3. On a clean work surface, using a rolling pin, roll out the dough to ⅛-inch thick. Cut out the dough with a cookie cutter and place the cut dough pieces on the prepared baking sheet, leaving about ½ inch between them.

4. In a small bowl, whisk the egg yolk with a fork. Brush the egg yolk over the dough and sprinkle with salt and flaxseed.

5. Bake for 10 to 12 minutes, until the cookies begin to brown. Transfer the cookies to a wire rack and let them cool completely.

6. Store the cookies in an airtight container at room temperature for up to 1 week.

If all else fails . . . If your kids are suspicious of toppings and mix-ins in their cookies, try skipping the ham and the flaxseed topping and call them "cheesy cookies." Because what kid doesn't love cheese?

SUPER GREEN FRITTATA BREAD

Serves 6 | **Prep time:** 15 minutes / **Cook time:** 50 minutes

NUT-FREE, VEGETARIAN, FREEZER-FRIENDLY

This savory homemade breakfast loaf is loaded with veggies and protein. Although it's a soft bread, you can easily slice and toast it in the morning or cut it into small cubes for little hands to enjoy.

½ cup extra-virgin olive
   oil, plus more for
   greasing the pan
2½ cups whole-wheat flour
¼ cup grated
   Parmesan cheese
1 teaspoon baking powder
½ teaspoon baking soda
¼ teaspoon sea salt
3 medium eggs
½ cup whole milk
½ cup frozen sweet peas
½ cup frozen
   shelled edamame
2 cups packed fresh baby
   spinach, roughly chopped
6 asparagus spears,
   trimmed and chopped
½ white onion, minced
4 fresh basil
   leaves, chopped

1. Preheat the oven to 400°F. Grease a 9-by-5-inch loaf pan with olive oil. Set aside.

2. In a large bowl mix together the flour, Parmesan cheese, baking powder, baking soda, and salt. Set aside.

3. In a separate large bowl, whisk together the eggs, milk, and oil.

4. Slowly add the dry ingredients to the wet ingredients and mix until the batter forms a very soft dough.

5. To make it more toddler-friendly: Set aside a handful of green peas to decorate the top of the bread in a fun polka-dot pattern.

6. Add the peas, edamame, spinach, asparagus, onion, and basil and mix until well combined. Transfer the batter to the prepared loaf pan. Decorate with the reserved peas (if using).

7. Bake for 50 minutes, until a toothpick inserted into the middle comes out clean. Let the bread cool in the pan for 10 minutes, then remove and let cool completely on a wire rack. Cut the bread into slices and serve.

8. To store, place parchment paper between leftover slices, wrap tightly in plastic wrap, and freeze for up to 4 months.

Swap it! Feel free to use whatever veggies you have on hand. Try kale, tomato, and zucchini for a change. Broccoli, mushrooms, and Swiss chard are a great combo, too.

BLUEBERRY YOGURT CAKE

Serves 6 | **Prep time:** 15 minutes / **Cook time:** 50 minutes
NUT-FREE, VEGETARIAN

This recipe is so easy to prepare that my 6-year-old makes it by himself while I lightly supervise. It is definitely a staple in my house. You can personalize the cake by making the base and changing the fruit to your toddler's favorite: strawberries, peaches, raspberries, apricots, chocolate, more vanilla, or simply plain yogurt all work really well.

¾ cup coconut oil, plus
  more for greasing the pan

3 medium eggs

½ cup coconut sugar

1½ cups plain Greek yogurt

1 teaspoon vanilla extract

2 cups whole-wheat flour

6 tablespoons
  tapioca starch

1 teaspoon baking soda

1 teaspoon baking powder

1 teaspoon sea salt

Zest of 1 medium orange

1 cup frozen blueberries

1. Preheat the oven to 400°F. Grease a springform Bundt pan with coconut oil.

2. In a large bowl, whisk the eggs and coconut sugar until the mixture is foamy and pale yellow. Add the yogurt, coconut oil, and vanilla and mix until combined.

3. In a separate large bowl, mix together the flour, tapioca starch, baking soda, baking powder, and salt.

4. Slowly add the dry ingredients to the wet ingredients and mix until combined. Add the orange zest and the blueberries and mix until combined.

5. Pour the batter into the prepared pan and bake for 50 minutes, or until a toothpick inserted into the middle comes out clean.

If all else fails . . . Sometimes your child just won't go for fruit, but chocolate never disappoints! Use chocolate chips instead of blueberries and add 2 tablespoons unsweetened cocoa powder to the dry ingredients. Your toddler will not say no.

WHOLE-GRAIN BANANA FRENCH TOAST STICKS

Serves 4 | **Prep time:** 5 minutes / **Cook time:** 10 minutes

DAIRY-FREE, NUT-FREE, VEGETARIAN, 30 MINUTES OR LESS, 5 INGREDIENTS OR LESS

This is a toddler version of traditional French toast. The bread is cut in to sticks so it's easy to grab. The banana adds nutrients and flavor.

4 medium eggs

2 ripe bananas, mashed

½ teaspoon ground cinnamon

4 whole-grain bread slices, each cut into 4 sticks

1 teaspoon butter

Maple syrup, for serving

Fresh fruit, for serving

1. In a shallow bowl, whisk the eggs. Add the mashed banana and the cinnamon and mix to combine.

2. Dredge each piece of bread in the egg mixture.

3. In a sauté pan or skillet over medium heat, melt the butter. Add the bread sticks to the pan and cook for 2 minutes on each side, until the bread is a golden brown and the eggs are fully cooked. Serve warm with maple syrup and fresh fruit on the side.

Swap it! Your toddler doesn't like banana? Use any other seasonal organic fruit that can be mashed into a purée. Apricots, plums, figs, and mangos are lovely options.

Polenta Pizza Squares, page 58

3

HANDHELDS FOR LITTLE HANDS

Toddlers love touching things, which is an important part of their development, as it supports language, cognitive skills, and motor skills. I consider eating finger food a sensory activity for little ones. They explore the texture, they smell, they taste, and they see the colors: All the senses are activated. In addition, using their little hands is way easier than using utensils and it's just more fun! This chapter offers easy-to-prepare and tasty handheld recipes that are great for the toddler in your home and for you, too. They are just right for school lunches or for taking along on a family trip. I've also made many of these recipes for parties where I like to serve finger food and single portions, so that the kids (and adults!) can easily help themselves.

Tomato Avocado Sandwiches 48

Smoked Salmon, Avocado, and Egg Sandwich Pockets 49

Zucchini and Ham Roll-Ups 50

Ham and Cheese Calzones 51

Roasted Broccoli and Ricotta Sandwiches 52

Focaccia Sandwiches with Bell Peppers, Ham, and Melted Cheese 53

Tomato and Cheese Tortilla Cups 54

Turkey, Tomato, and Pesto Pita Pockets 55

Beef and Zucchini Baked Samosas 56

Polenta Pizza Squares 58

Easy Phyllo Pizzas 59

Healthy Beef and Veggie Burgers 61

TOMATO AVOCADO SANDWICHES

Serves 4 | **Prep time:** 10 minutes

DAIRY-FREE, NUT-FREE, 30 MINUTES OR LESS, 5 INGREDIENTS OR LESS

This is one of our favorite sandwich combinations. When heirloom tomatoes are in season and you can taste the sun and the sweetness in their pulp, there is nothing better for a light lunch for the whole family. Hass avocados are my favorite variety, because they are so creamy and tasty. Avocados also provide a high amount of omega-3 fatty acids—brain fuel for the kids.

5 slices multigrain bread

3 tablespoons mayonnaise

2 heirloom tomatoes, cored and sliced

Pinch sea salt

2 Hass avocados, peeled, pitted, and sliced

1. Toast the bread slices in a toaster to your desired doneness. For toddlers, the bread should not be too crispy or hard.

2. For an adult sandwich, spread ½ tablespoon mayonnaise on 1 slice of toast. Top with tomato slices and sprinkle with salt. Layer the avocado slices on top. Spread ½ tablespoon mayonnaise on the second slice and complete the sandwich.

3. To make it more toddler-friendly: Spread 1 tablespoon mayonnaise on 1 slice of toast and cut it in half. Layer the tomato and avocado on one half and top with the other half. Cut the sandwich into even smaller pieces so it can be held by little fingers.

If all else fails . . . Like my own child, some toddlers don't like their foods mixed together in a sandwich. What works for my son is a "deconstructed" sandwich—I simply place the sandwich parts next to each other on his plate. It's impressive to see him eating everything if I display the food in a different way. It really works!

SMOKED SALMON, AVOCADO, AND EGG SANDWICH POCKETS

Serves 4 | **Prep time:** 15 minutes

DAIRY-FREE, NUT-FREE, 30 MINUTES OR LESS, 5 INGREDIENTS OR LESS

You will only need a round cookie cutter or a drinking glass to transform a regular sandwich into a sandwich pocket. These sandwich pockets resemble ravioli and are filled with omega-3 fatty acids and proteins. To top it off, they taste great!

1 Hass avocado, peeled, pitted, and roughly chopped

2 hard-boiled eggs, roughly chopped

3 tablespoons mayonnaise

Pinch sea salt

8 slices whole-wheat bread

2 slices smoked salmon, shredded

1. Have a small bowl of water ready.

2. In a medium bowl, mash together the avocado, eggs, and mayonnaise until it forms a chunky paste. Season with the salt. Set aside.

3. *To make it more toddler-friendly:* Put the avocado, hard-boiled eggs, mayonnaise, smoked salmon, salt, and bread in a food processor and purée until smooth.

4. Using a 3½-inch round cookie cutter or a drinking glass, cut a circle from each bread slice. Add 1 or 2 teaspoons of the egg mixture in the center of each piece of bread and top with 1 teaspoon shredded salmon.

5. Dip your finger into the bowl of water and moisten the perimeter of the circle of bread. Place a second circle of bread on top. The water will help seal the pockets. Gently press the edge of the circle to seal in the filling. Press the tines of a fork around the edge to create a pretty crimped look.

Prep help: What to do with the bread scraps? Cut them in cubes, season with a pinch of salt, dried oregano or thyme, and a drizzle of olive oil. Toast them in a 400°F oven for 15 minutes, turning them once, until browned. They will become super tasty croutons for your next salad.

ZUCCHINI AND HAM ROLL-UPS

Serves 4 | **Prep time:** 15 minutes / **Cook time:** 5 minutes

EGG-FREE, GLUTEN-FREE, NUT-FREE, 30 MINUTES OR LESS, 5 INGREDIENTS OR LESS

These sushi-style rolls are filled with grilled zucchini and ham and a lovely layer of cream cheese to hold everything together. To save time, you can grill the zucchini in advance and store it in an airtight container in the refrigerator for up to 4 days. If you don't have a gas or charcoal grill, you can cook the zucchini on the stovetop in a skillet or grill pan. I like to buy ham that is processed without nitrites, nitrates, or polyphosphates.

1 zucchini, cut into long, thin slices

1 tablespoon extra-virgin olive oil

Pinch sea salt

2 tablespoons cream cheese

3 slices whole-grain flatbread

3 slices cooked ham

1. Preheat a gas grill or prepare a charcoal grill.

2. Rub the zucchini slices all over with the oil. Grill the zucchini for 2 minutes on each side. For adult portions, season with the salt. Set aside the zucchini.

3. Spread a generous ½ tablespoon cream cheese on each slice of flatbread. Place 1 slice of ham and 2 slices of grilled zucchini in the center of each flatbread. Roll up each flatbread and cut them crosswise into thick slices. Use a fun food pick to hold the roll together, if needed.

Swap it! If your toddler doesn't like zucchini, you can easily substitute it with some baby spinach or sweet red or yellow bell peppers.

HAM AND CHEESE CALZONES

Serves 6 | **Prep time:** 15 minutes / **Cook time:** 18 to 20 minutes
EGG-FREE, NUT-FREE, 5 INGREDIENTS OR LESS

Since they were little, my kids have been helping me prepare pizza, because they love playing with the dough. When they were toddlers, I gave them a small piece of dough to play with while I made the "big" pizza for everyone. Now they choose the toppings from a selection I offer them and they prepare their own individual pizzas. Calzones are very much like pizza but with the filling on the inside. I think this recipe is more toddler-friendly, because of the taste and because calzones are easy to hold in small hands.

14 ounces pizza
   dough, homemade or
   store-bought
Semolina flour or
   all-purpose flour,
   for dusting
4 ounces provolone
   cheese, diced
6 slices cooked ham, cut
   into small pieces
4 tablespoons extra-virgin
   olive oil

1. Preheat the oven to 400°F. Line a baking sheet with parchment paper. Set aside.

2. Cut the pizza dough into 8 pieces. Dust a clean work surface with some semolina flour. Using your hands, shape each piece of dough into a flat, round circle. The flour will keep the dough from sticking.

3. Place a few pieces of cheese and a few pieces of ham in the center of each piece of dough. For adults, you can always add other ingredients, like black olives, mushrooms, or sun-dried tomatoes.

4. Gently fold the dough over the filling and press the edges with your fingers to seal.

5. Place the calzones on the prepared baking sheet and brush with oil.

6. Bake for 18 to 20 minutes, until browned. Serve warm for adults, and allow the calzones to cool before cutting into bite-size pieces and serving to toddlers.

Swap it! Because everyone can have their own calzone, everyone can have a different one filled with their favorite foods.

ROASTED BROCCOLI AND RICOTTA SANDWICHES

Serves 4 | **Prep time:** 15 minutes / **Cook time:** 25 minutes

EGG-FREE, NUT-FREE, VEGETARIAN, 5 INGREDIENTS OR LESS

Veggies and cheese are a great toddler-friendly combination. In this sandwich, broccoli and ricotta are combined into a smooth and delicate cream that becomes a delicious spread for the sandwich. The broccoli can be roasted in advance and stored in an airtight container in the refrigerator for up to 2 days.

½ medium head broccoli, cut into florets, stems discarded

3 tablespoons extra-virgin olive oil

1 teaspoon dried thyme

Pinch sea salt

2 tablespoons ricotta cheese

¼ teaspoon ground nutmeg

8 slices bread with sesame seeds

Cherry tomatoes (optional)

1 carrot, peeled and cut into thick slices (optional)

1 cucumber, cut into thick slices (optional)

1. Preheat the oven to 400°F. Line a baking sheet with parchment paper.

2. Place the broccoli florets on the prepared baking sheet and toss with the oil, thyme, and salt.

3. Roast for 25 minutes, turning once, until cooked through. Let cool.

4. In a food processor, process the roasted broccoli, ricotta cheese, and nutmeg until smooth.

5. Spread the ricotta-broccoli mixture onto 4 of the bread slices and top with the remaining 4 slices to make sandwiches.

6. To make it more toddler-friendly: Cut a sandwich into 1-inch squares and slide the squares onto a child-safe food pick with veggies they enjoy, like cherry tomatoes or carrot and cucumber slices.

If all else fails . . . Ricotta has a mild, delicate flavor. If your toddler likes a cheesier flavor, use cream cheese instead and add 1 tablespoon grated Parmesan cheese to the mixture. Proceed with the recipe as instructed.

FOCACCIA SANDWICHES WITH BELL PEPPERS, HAM, AND MELTED CHEESE

Serves 4 | **Prep time:** 20 minutes / **Cook time:** 25 minutes
EGG-FREE, NUT-FREE, 5 INGREDIENTS OR LESS

The softness of the focaccia bread and the flavor of the olive oil make this a kid favorite. Whenever I find good focaccia, I like to use it for our sandwiches. Bell peppers, ham, and provolone are a great combo with this kind of bread.

2 small red or yellow bell peppers, stemmed, seeded, and cut in half lengthwise

4 (4-by-5-inch) slices focaccia

4 slices smoked provolone cheese

Extra-virgin olive oil, for drizzling

Pinch sea salt

4 slices cooked ham

1. Preheat the oven to 450°F. Line a rimmed baking sheet with parchment paper. Have a toaster oven or panini maker ready.

2. Place the bell peppers, cut-side down, on the prepared baking sheet. Roast for 25 minutes. The skins will wrinkle. Place the peppers in a bowl, cover, and let rest for 10 minutes. Peel the skin off the peppers and discard. Cut the peppers into thin strips.

3. Cut each slice of focaccia in half horizontally. Place 1 slice of cheese and a few strips of bell pepper on a slice of focaccia. Drizzle with olive oil and sprinkle with salt. Add 1 slice of ham, and top with the other half of the focaccia. Repeat to make 4 sandwiches.

4. Toast each sandwich for a few minutes in the panini maker or toaster oven, until the cheese melts.

5. To make it more toddler-friendly: Cut the sandwiches into strips or squares to serve for little hands.

Swap it! Your little one doesn't like bell peppers? Try zucchini. You don't eat ham? Make these sandwiches with turkey or chicken.

TOMATO AND CHEESE TORTILLA CUPS

Serves 6 | **Prep time:** 15 minutes / **Cook time:** 10 minutes
EGG-FREE, NUT-FREE, VEGETARIAN, 30 MINUTES OR LESS

This is such a fun lunch idea! Kids love the cup shape and they really like the crunchy texture of the tortillas. They also make delicious appetizers for a party. To serve them, place the cups on a tray with the tomato salad next to it, so guests can fill the cup with the tomatoes right before they eat them, which will keep the crunchiness.

6 (12-inch) flour tortillas

4 tablespoons extra-virgin
   olive oil, divided

1 teaspoon fresh
   thyme, minced

4 sage leaves, minced

¼ teaspoon sea
   salt, divided

3 heirloom
   tomatoes, chopped

½ cup crumbled
   Manchego cheese

½ cup frozen corn, thawed

1 teaspoon
   balsamic vinegar

1. Preheat the oven to 400°F.

2. With a 4-inch round cookie cutter, cut 2 circles from each tortilla. Place the circles into a 12-cup muffin tin.

3. In a small cup, mix together 2 tablespoons olive oil, the thyme, sage, and ⅛ teaspoon salt. Brush the inside of each tortilla cup with the oil mixture.

4. Bake for 10 minutes, until the tortillas are firm. Let cool.

5. In a large bowl, mix together the tomatoes, cheese, and corn. In a small bowl, whisk together the remaining 2 tablespoons oil, balsamic vinegar, and the remaining ⅛ teaspoon salt. Pour it over the tomato salad and toss to mix.

6. Fill the tortilla cups with the tomato salad and serve 2 cups to each person.

Prep help: To save time, bake the tortilla cups in advance and fill them when you are ready to serve. They can be stored at room temperature on a plate covered with a kitchen towel to keep them crispy.

TURKEY, TOMATO, AND PESTO PITA POCKETS

Serves 4 | **Prep time:** 15 minutes

DAIRY-FREE, EGG-FREE, 30 MINUTES OR LESS, 5 INGREDIENTS OR LESS

In Greece, we used to enjoy pita filled with meat, veggies, and sauce, which was rolled into a cone like an ice cream. Super good but very messy, even for adults. That's why I like to cut the pita in half for little hands and fill the inside like a pocket. The kids will be able to hold the pita and eat it without dropping food all over the place.

1 heirloom
   tomato, chopped

4 turkey slices, cut
   into strips

3 tablespoons basil pesto

4 whole-grain pitas, each
   cut in half

1. In a small bowl, mix together the tomato, turkey, and pesto.

2. Carefully open the pita to create a pocket, fill with the turkey and tomato mixture, and serve each person 2 pockets.

If all else fails . . . If your little one doesn't like pesto, try mixing the tomatoes and turkey with mayonnaise or ranch dressing.

BEEF AND ZUCCHINI BAKED SAMOSAS

Serves 4 | **Prep time:** 15 minutes / **Cook time:** 35 minutes
DAIRY-FREE, EGG-FREE, NUT-FREE, FREEZER-FRIENDLY

Samosas are savory pastries that are either fried or baked. Their small size makes them great for kids. These are filled with zucchini and ground beef and baked in the oven, which is a lighter and healthier option than deep-frying. The zucchini keeps them moist while adding some extra nutrients. Folding the phyllo is a little like folding origami. Have your toddler watch while you show how a big rectangle of phyllo transforms into a triangular samosa. The kids can help you fill them.

2 tablespoons extra-virgin
  olive oil, plus ¼ cup,
  for brushing
3 scallions, minced
1 garlic clove, minced
½ pound ground beef
1 zucchini, diced
1 medium yellow
  squash, diced
Pinch sea salt
3 tablespoons
  breadcrumbs
4 fresh mint leaves, minced
8 sheets phyllo
  pastry, thawed

1. Preheat the oven to 400°F. Line a baking sheet with parchment paper.

2. In a large sauté pan or skillet over medium heat, warm 2 tablespoons olive oil. Add the scallions and garlic and cook, stirring often, until golden, about 3 minutes. Add the ground beef, zucchini, and yellow squash and stir well.

3. Season with salt and reduce the heat to low. Cover and simmer for 10 minutes.

4. Add the breadcrumbs and mint and stir well. Let cool.

5. Unroll the phyllo, remove 1 sheet, and lay it on a clean work surface. Re-roll the remaining phyllo and cover with a damp towel so it won't dry out.

6. Brush the phyllo with olive oil. Fold the top of the phyllo down to make a 9-by-9-inch square. Brush again with oil.

7. Fold up the lower right corner to create a triangle. Brush with oil.

8. Fold the top right corner down toward the left until about 1 inch of the point extends over the edge. Fold the lower left corner on top of it. You should have a cone-like pocket.

9. Carefully open the pocket and fill with 2 tablespoons of the zucchini-beef mixture. Close the pocket by folding over the excess phyllo and brush with olive oil to seal everything. Repeat with the rest of the phyllo and filling.

10. Place the samosas on the prepared baking sheet, brush with olive oil, and bake for 15 to 20 minutes, until golden brown. Serve 2 per person, warm or at room temperature.

Swap it! Looking for a vegetarian filling? Skip the beef and add more veggies, like carrots, sweet peas, broccoli, or even some tofu for a little added protein.

POLENTA PIZZA SQUARES

Serves 4 | **Prep time:** 15 minutes / **Cook time:** 15 minutes
EGG-FREE, GLUTEN-FREE, NUT-FREE, VEGETARIAN, 30 MINUTES OR LESS

If you are looking for a naturally gluten-free pizza option, you'll like this recipe. Easy to prepare and kid-approved, you can play around with the toppings just like you would for traditional pizza. The difference between "instant" polenta or "regular" polenta is that instant polenta has been steamed and precooked to greatly reduce the cooking time from 45 to 60 minutes to 10 to 15 minutes, which means that making polenta on weeknights is a viable option. To speed up the cooling time for the polenta, place it in the refrigerator for 10 minutes and it will be ready to use.

4 cups water

Pinch sea salt

1 cup instant polenta

3 tablespoons tomato sauce

4½ ounces mozzarella, diced

1 cup cherry tomatoes, each cut in half

1 cup packed baby spinach

8 Taggiasca olives, each cut in half

1 tablespoon dried oregano

2 tablespoons extra-virgin olive oil

1. Fill a pot with the water, add the salt, and bring to a boil over high heat. Add the polenta, lower the heat to medium, and whisk for 5 minutes, until the polenta starts to thicken. Cook for 5 more minutes, stirring frequently. Remove from the heat and let cool for 3 minutes.

2. Preheat the oven to 450°F. Line a baking sheet with parchment paper.

3. Transfer the polenta to a clean work surface, spread it out to 1-inch thick, and let it cool completely.

4. With a sharp knife, cut the polenta into 2½-inch, toddler-size squares and place them on the prepared baking sheet.

5. Spread ½ teaspoon tomato sauce on each square and top with a few pieces of mozzarella, 1 or 2 cherry tomatoes, 1 baby spinach leaf, ½ olive, and a sprinkle of oregano. Drizzle with olive oil.

6. Bake for 5 minutes, until the mozzarella melts. Serve warm, or cooled to room temperature for toddlers.

Make it fun. Have your toddler help you cut out the polenta using cookie cutters in fun shapes. Don't worry about wasting the scraps. Polenta is like Play-Doh: combine the scraps together, re-roll them, and cut out more shapes.

EASY PHYLLO PIZZAS

Serves 4 | **Prep time:** 10 minutes / **Cook time:** 15 minutes

EGG-FREE, NUT-FREE, VEGETARIAN, 30 MINUTES OR LESS, FREEZER-FRIENDLY

Toddlers + pizza = love at first sight. If you don't have time to prepare a traditional pizza dough, phyllo pastry offers a crispy and flaky shortcut. If your toddlers love art projects, this is a good recipe to get them involved. They can brush the phyllo pastry with olive oil. I find that 5 sheets of phyllo are enough for this recipe, but if you prefer a crunchier result, use as many as 10 sheets. The little ones can also help by adding the toppings to the pizza. If you let them pick which vegetables to add, they are much more likely to eat them.

7 tablespoons extra-virgin olive oil, divided

5 to 10 sheets phyllo pastry, thawed

¾ cup tomato sauce

Pinch sea salt

1 heirloom tomato, cored and cut into ¼-inch slices

1 small zucchini, thinly sliced

16 ounces mozzarella cheese, diced

1 tablespoon pitted chopped black olives

5 fresh basil leaves

1. Preheat the oven to 425°F. Grease a 9-by-13-inch baking dish with 2 tablespoons olive oil. Pour 3 tablespoons olive oil into a small cup for brushing.

2. Place 1 sheet of phyllo in the baking dish and brush with olive oil. Place a second phyllo sheet over the first and brush with olive oil. Repeat until you have 5 sheets (or more if you want a crispier pizza).

3. Spread the tomato sauce on the phyllo. Sprinkle with salt and top with the tomatoes, zucchini, mozzarella, olives, and basil. Drizzle the remaining 2 tablespoons olive oil over the top and bake for 15 minutes, until the mozzarella is melted and lightly golden.

4. Cut the pizza into 4-inch squares and serve.

Swap it! You don't have time to prepare pizza dough and your toddler doesn't want the "weird" phyllo pastry? Use pita bread as a base.

HEALTHY BEEF AND VEGGIE BURGERS

Serves 4 | **Prep time:** 20 minutes / **Cook time:** 10 minutes

NUT-FREE, 30 MINUTES OR LESS, FREEZER-FRIENDLY

These juicy burgers are loaded with veggies and served on buns with avocado, tomato, lettuce, and mayonnaise, so you can feel good about burger night. This recipe makes four full-size burgers, or you can make eight half-size burgers with mini buns. I love to make the burger patties ahead of time and freeze them. Then, when a crazy busy week rolls around, all I have to do is place the patties in the refrigerator overnight to thaw and dinner comes together in a flash.

1 pound ground beef

1 zucchini, finely grated and drained

1 small carrot, peeled and finely grated

½ cup minced cremini mushrooms

2 tablespoons grated Parmesan cheese

3 tablespoons minced yellow onion

1 garlic clove, minced

1 teaspoon dried oregano

Pinch sea salt

4 tablespoons mayonnaise

4 regular-size hamburger buns or 8 mini-hamburger buns

4 lettuce leaves

2 yellow heirloom tomatoes, cored and sliced

2 Hass avocados, peeled, cored, and sliced

1. In a large bowl, mix together the ground beef, zucchini, carrot, mushrooms, Parmesan cheese, onion, garlic, oregano, and salt.

2. Form the mixture into 4 full patties or 8 kid-size patties. You can choose to grill the patties or freeze them by placing them in an airtight container with parchment between each patty so they don't stick together.

3. In a grill pan over medium-high heat, cook the burgers a few at a time, leaving some space in between, until the top of the patty starts to darken in color. Flip and cook for a few minutes longer. Do not press on the patty while it's cooking or the juices will run out.

4. Spread 1 tablespoon mayonnaise on each bun.

5. Assemble the burgers in this order: bun, mayonnaise, lettuce, tomato, burger, avocado, bun. Enjoy!

6. **To make it more toddler-friendly:** Cut a burger into quarters and serve with a dipping sauce like Healthy Tomato Ketchup on page 136.

Make it fun. Make monster burgers! Slice a zucchini lengthwise and place 1 long slice on the burger when you assemble them. Cut 2 small cheese circles and place them next to each other on top of the bun. Cut a black olive in half and place 1 on each piece of cheese to make eyes.

Fennel Leek Soup with Parmesan Chips, page 66

4

VEGETABLES YOUR KIDS WILL (MIGHT) EAT

Of all the foods, vegetables always seem to be the least appealing to toddlers. Maybe it's the texture—some can be very fibrous, the low sugar (that's why carrots and sweet potatoes, the sweetest of vegetables, generally avoid the blacklist), or the outsized expectations of parents who are trying to get their kids to eat nutritious food. What worked with my kids was our neutral approach to vegetables. I added them to every recipe, talked about why each one was good for them, but most of all, I did not use them as an obligation to get a reward (if you eat your veggies, you can have dessert). The recipes in this chapter are all vegetarian and call for seasonal and organic produce. Every recipe focuses on a different vegetable, but I'm a big believer in swapping out ingredients if needed. If your little one doesn't like a particular vegetable, switch it for one they do like.

Quinoa Veggie Croquettes 64

Vegetable Minestrone 65

Fennel Leek Soup with Parmesan Chips 66

Cream of Carrot and Lentil Soup 67

Cucumber, Tomato, Mango, and Avocado Salad 69

Purple Cabbage Potato Salad 70

Parmesan Roasted Asparagus and Butternut Squash 71

Spaghetti and Zoodles 72

Red Lentil and Vegetable Bowl 73

Eggplant, Tomato, and Feta Pasta 74

Broccoli Risotto 75

Baked Spinach Pasta Casserole 76

QUINOA VEGGIE CROQUETTES

Serves 4 | **Prep time:** 15 minutes / **Cook time:** 20 minutes
NUT-FREE, VEGETARIAN

To prepare these lovely croquettes, the vegetables are pulsed in a food processor until the texture is the same as the quinoa. The eggs and flour hold everything together. These little croquettes are the perfect addition to any lunch box!

½ cup quinoa, rinsed under
   running water
1 cup water
¾ teaspoon sea
   salt, divided
1 cup broccoli florets
1 cup chopped carrots
1 cup chopped zucchini
3 tablespoons
   whole-wheat flour
⅓ cup grated
   Parmesan cheese
¼ teaspoon garlic powder
2 medium eggs
3 tablespoons extra-virgin
   olive oil

1. In a medium saucepan, mix together the quinoa, water, and ¼ teaspoon salt and bring to a boil over high heat. Reduce the heat to medium-low, cover, and simmer until tender, 12 minutes. Set aside.

2. In a food processor, add the broccoli florets, carrots, and zucchini and pulse in 5-second intervals, until the mixture has the texture of breadcrumbs.

3. To make it more toddler-friendly: Continue to pulse until the vegetables are as small as grains of sand.

4. In a large bowl, mix together the quinoa, pulsed vegetables, flour, Parmesan cheese, garlic powder, eggs, and the remaining ½ teaspoon salt.

5. Line a serving plate with paper towels.

6. In a large skillet over medium heat, warm the olive oil for 30 seconds and swirl to coat the pan.

7. Shape 1 tablespoon of the mixture into a croquette (or any shape you like) with your hands. Place it in the pan. Repeat with the rest of the mixture. Leave space between the croquettes as you will need to flip them—you may need to cook them in batches. Cook until golden brown, about 4 minutes on each side.

8. Transfer to the paper towel–lined plate to drain any excess oil. Serve warm, or cooled to room temperature for toddlers.

Make it fun. Have fun shaping these croquettes with your kids–into hearts, triangles, patties, whatever you like!

VEGETABLE MINESTRONE

Serves 6 | **Prep time:** 20 minutes / **Cook time:** 20 minutes
DAIRY-FREE, EGG-FREE, GLUTEN-FREE, NUT-FREE, VEGAN, ONE-POT

Minestrone is such a versatile recipe: You can mix and match nearly any vegetables that you like. I include at least five or six different vegetables, depending on what's in season and what I have in the refrigerator. Because the vegetables change every time I make it, the final flavor is always something new and interesting. For this recipe, I've selected vegetables that you can find any time of the year with reliable and delicious results. It's fine to use pre-cut frozen vegetables to save time.

½ head cauliflower, cut
  into florets

3 zucchinis, thickly sliced

3 small potatoes, chopped

2 medium carrots, peeled
  and roughly chopped

2 cups packed
  fresh spinach

1 leek, chopped

1 yellow onion, chopped

2 garlic cloves, chopped

1 sprig fresh rosemary

1 tablespoon sea salt

¼ cup extra-virgin olive oil,
  for serving (optional)

¼ cup grated Parmesan
  cheese, for serving
  (optional)

1. In a large pot, mix together the cauliflower, zucchinis, potatoes, carrots, spinach, leek, onion, garlic, rosemary, and salt. Add enough water to barely cover the vegetables and bring to a boil over high heat. Reduce the heat to medium-low and simmer until the vegetables are tender, about 20 minutes.

2. Remove and discard the rosemary sprig. Serve the minestrone warm with a drizzle of olive oil and sprinkled with 1 tablespoon Parmesan cheese (if using).

3. **To make it more toddler-friendly:** Purée the soup in the pot using an immersion blender before serving.

If all else fails . . . Toddlers love pasta! To make this soup even more toddler-friendly, add some small pasta, like ditalini or elbows. Cook the pasta in a separate pot, drain it, and add it to individual bowls of the minestrone.

FENNEL LEEK SOUP WITH PARMESAN CHIPS

Serves 4 | **Prep time:** 10 minutes / **Cook time:** 30 minutes

EGG-FREE, GLUTEN-FREE, NUT-FREE, VEGETARIAN, ONE-POT

Here is one of the easiest and most delicious soups you can prepare that the whole family will enjoy. The fennel provides a light, fresh licorice flavor that is perfectly balanced by the cheesy and salty Parmesan. A word of warning: The Parmesan chips are addictive for toddlers and adults!

3 cups vegetable broth

1 medium fennel bulb, trimmed and thickly sliced

2 leeks, sliced

2 garlic cloves, chopped

1 tablespoon minced fresh thyme

½ teaspoon sea salt

1 cup grated Parmesan cheese

2 tablespoons extra-virgin olive oil, for serving

1. Preheat the oven to 450°F. Line a baking sheet with parchment paper.

2. In a large pot over high heat, mix together the broth, fennel, leeks, garlic, thyme, and salt, and bring to a boil. Reduce the heat to medium-low and simmer until the vegetables are tender, about 20 minutes. Remove from the heat.

3. Spoon the Parmesan cheese onto the baking sheet, 1 tablespoon at a time, in small piles, leaving a little space between each pile.

4. Bake for 8 minutes until the cheese melts. Let cool completely.

5. Using an immersion blender, purée the soup until smooth.

6. Serve the soup warm with a drizzle of olive oil and a few Parmesan chips on top.

7. To make it more toddler-friendly: Serve the soup in a small cup with Parmesan chips on the side. Tell them the soup is a "sauce" for the chips. How much sauce can they scoop up with each chip?

Prep help: You can prepare the Parmesan chips ahead and store them in an airtight container in the refrigerator. I usually place a paper towel in the container, which helps prevent the chips from getting soggy.

CREAM OF CARROT AND LENTIL SOUP

Serves 4 | **Prep time:** 10 minutes / **Cook time:** 30 minutes

DAIRY-FREE, EGG-FREE, GLUTEN-FREE, NUT-FREE, VEGAN, ONE-POT

For a gentle way to introduce spices to your toddler, try giving them this creamy soup. The cumin and turmeric quietly complement the lentils and coconut, and (bonus!) it's ready in half an hour. To complete the meal, brown rice would be a lovely side for this dish. Unless your toddler is adventurous with their food, I would skip the parsley, kale, and sunflower seeds.

1 cup red lentils

3 tablespoons extra-virgin olive oil

1 red onion, minced

1 garlic clove, minced

1 pound carrots, peeled and thinly sliced

1 teaspoon ground cumin

1 teaspoon ground turmeric

Pinch sea salt

4 cups vegetable broth

1 cup coconut cream

1 tablespoon minced fresh parsley

3 to 5 kale leaves, stems removed and roughly chopped

2 tablespoons sunflower seeds

1. Rinse the lentils under running water and set aside.

2. In a large pot over medium heat, mix together the olive oil, onion, and garlic and cook until the onion is softened, about 2 minutes. Add the carrots, cumin, turmeric, and salt and cook for 4 minutes. Add the lentils and broth, cover, and simmer until the lentils are tender, about 20 minutes (or follow the cooking time on the lentil package).

3. Remove the pot from the heat and mix in the coconut cream.

4. To make it more toddler-friendly: Purée the soup with an immersion blender until smooth.

5. Add the parsley and kale and stir to combine. Sprinkle the sunflower seeds on top and serve warm for adults and lukewarm for kids.

Make it fun. Whenever I give my kids soup, I always put it in a bowl with a fun animal design on the bottom of the bowl. I'll tell them a story about a hidden animal they have to "discover" by emptying their bowl. They love it.

CUCUMBER, TOMATO, MANGO, AND AVOCADO SALAD

Serves 4 | **Prep time:** 15 minutes

DAIRY-FREE, EGG-FREE, GLUTEN-FREE, NUT-FREE, VEGAN, 30 MINUTES OR LESS

Conventional salads are not super toddler-friendly: They are not so easy to eat, the pieces are too big, and the flavors can be acidic. I've "toddlerized" salad by using mild, creamy, and comforting flavors like mango and avocado and cutting the ingredients into kid-size pieces. It's a real game-changer and the whole family will love it.

4 tablespoons extra-virgin olive oil

1 tablespoon apple cider vinegar

½ teaspoon sea salt

3 fresh mint leaves, minced

3 fresh basil leaves, minced

4 medium Persian cucumbers, diced

4 medium Japanese tomatoes, firm, diced

2 medium Hass avocados, peeled, pitted, and diced

1 mango, peeled, pitted, and diced

1. To make the dressing, in a small cup, whisk together the olive oil, vinegar, salt, mint, and basil until it is creamy and emulsified.

2. In a large bowl, mix together the cucumbers, tomatoes, avocado, and mango. Pour the dressing over the salad and gently toss to combine. Serve immediately.

Make it fun. Don't throw away the avocado shells. Spoon the salad into each one and serve them to your kids as salad boats. They will love them!

PURPLE CABBAGE POTATO SALAD

Serves 6 | **Prep time:** 10 minutes / **Cook time:** 15 minutes
DAIRY-FREE, EGG-FREE, GLUTEN-FREE, NUT-FREE, VEGAN, 30 MINUTES OR LESS, 5 INGREDIENTS OR LESS

This salad is crunchy and creamy at the same time, and it's at its best when served warm. Mix the potatoes with the cabbage as soon as you drain them from the pot: The heat of the potatoes will make the cabbage tender enough to be easily digested. Kids will love the purple color of the cabbage and how it dyes the potatoes. You can buy balsamic vinegar reduction at most grocery stores.

5 medium russet potatoes, peeled and cut into small cubes

½ medium red cabbage, very thinly sliced

5 tablespoons extra-virgin olive oil

1 tablespoon balsamic vinegar reduction

1 teaspoon sea salt

1. Bring a large pot of water to a boil. Add the potatoes and cook until tender, about 15 minutes.

2. Transfer the potatoes to a large bowl and immediately toss with the cabbage.

3. To make the dressing, in a small bowl, whisk together the olive oil, balsamic reduction, and salt. Pour over the salad and gently toss to combine. Serve warm, or cooled to room temperature for toddlers.

If all else fails . . . This recipe has a 1:1 ratio of cabbage to potatoes. If you are just introducing cabbage to your little one and you encounter some resistance, reduce the cabbage quantity to a 1:2 ratio. You can slowly increase it later on.

PARMESAN ROASTED ASPARAGUS AND BUTTERNUT SQUASH

Serves 4 | **Prep time:** 10 minutes / **Cook time:** 30 minutes

EGG-FREE, GLUTEN-FREE, NUT-FREE, VEGETARIAN, ONE-POT, 5 INGREDIENTS OR LESS

Asparagus and butternut squash are such a great combination. They are both so bright-colored that kids love how they look and the flavors go well together. This recipe is made in a sheet pan and requires only 10 minutes of prep—the rest of the time is spent roasting in the oven. Serve with a side of brown rice or quinoa. If asparagus is not available at the store, use green beans or broccoli instead.

1 pound
   asparagus, chopped

1 butternut squash, peeled
   and diced

1 garlic clove, minced

3 tablespoons extra-virgin
   olive oil

½ teaspoon sea salt

½ cup grated
   Parmesan cheese

1. Preheat the oven to 400°F. Line a baking sheet with parchment paper.

2. Place the asparagus, butternut squash, and garlic on the baking sheet and drizzle with olive oil and sprinkle with the salt. Toss the mixture well with a spoon to coat the vegetables. Sprinkle the Parmesan cheese on top.

3. Bake for 25 minutes, stirring once halfway through the baking time. Turn the oven to broil and bake for 5 more minutes, until golden.

   If all else fails . . . Don't think the cheese will be enough to entice your little one to eat the veggies? Create a coating using a mix of half Parmesan cheese and half breadcrumbs and coat the veggies with it before baking. The kids will love the crunchy goodness.

SPAGHETTI AND ZOODLES

Serves 6 | **Prep time:** 15 minutes / **Cook time:** 20 minutes
EGG-FREE, NUT-FREE, VEGETARIAN

If you are looking for a super easy summer recipe that will combine mom or dad's goal of losing some weight (or just not gaining any) and the kids' need for a well-balanced and delicious meal, you've come to the right place. If you prepare the tomato sauce ahead of time and freeze it so it's ready to use, the whole recipe can be ready in the time it takes to cook the pasta. If you don't have a spiralizer, you can use a vegetable peeler and peel long, thin ribbons from the zucchini—a vegetable tagliatelle instead of spaghetti.

1 pound spaghetti

3 tablespoons extra-virgin olive oil

1 garlic clove, minced

2 large tomatoes, diced

1½ teaspoons dried oregano

Pinch sea salt

2 zucchinis, spiralized

4 tablespoons grated Parmesan cheese, for serving

1. Fill a large pot with water and bring to a boil. Cook the pasta according to the package directions. Reserve ½ cup of the pasta water.

2. In a medium saucepan over medium-high heat, warm the olive oil. Add the garlic and cook for 1 minute. Add the tomatoes and stir to combine.

3. Add the oregano and salt, stir to combine, and cook for 10 to 12 minutes, until the flavors blend.

4. To make it more toddler-friendly: Use an immersion blender to purée the sauce.

5. In a large bowl, mix together the zucchini zoodles, spaghetti, and the tomato sauce until combined. The heat from the pasta and the tomato sauce will be enough to make the zucchini nicely tender. If the sauce seems too thick, add a little of the reserved pasta water.

6. Serve warm, or cooled to room temperature for toddlers, with grated Parmesan cheese sprinkled over the top.

If all else fails . . . If your little one is in a "no suspicious colors" phase, you can dress the pasta with some extra-virgin olive oil or butter and use yellow squash instead of the green zucchini.

RED LENTIL AND VEGETABLE BOWL

Serves 4 | **Prep time:** 15 minutes / **Cook time:** 30 minutes

EGG-FREE, GLUTEN-FREE, NUT-FREE, VEGAN, ONE-POT

Earthy and loaded with comforting flavors and nutrients, this soup is a good choice to serve on a cold day. All the ingredients are chopped into bite-size pieces, perfect for toddlers, so you won't need to purée the soup. Did you ever play the "Guess what's inside?" game with your kids? Ask them to look in their soup and try to guess the ingredients. Hints are welcome. You can even set a prize for the winner. To save time, I place the garlic and onion in a food processor and pulse for a few seconds. Next, I pulse the carrots, cabbage, and kale. I pulse the potatoes into small pieces last.

¼ cup extra-virgin olive oil

1 small white onion, minced

2 garlic cloves, minced

1 cup red lentils

½ red cabbage, shredded

4 small russet potatoes, peeled and chopped

2 carrots, peeled and chopped

5 cups vegetable broth

2 bay leaves

1½ teaspoons sea salt

8 to 10 kale leaves, stems removed and leaves chopped

1. In a large pot over medium heat, warm the olive oil. Add the onion and garlic and cook until golden, 2 to 3 minutes.

2. Rinse the lentils under running water and add them to the pot. Add the cabbage, potatoes, carrots, and vegetable broth to the pot. Add the bay leaves and salt, stir to combine, and bring to a boil. Reduce the heat to medium-low and simmer for 20 minutes.

3. Add the kale and cook for an additional 5 minutes. Serve warm, or cooled to room temperature for toddlers.

If all else fails . . . Parmesan cheese is such a recipe-saver. When I top this soup with a generous tablespoon of grated Parmesan cheese, the kids handle the spoon with new energy.

EGGPLANT, TOMATO, AND FETA PASTA

Serves 4 | **Prep time:** 15 minutes / **Cook time:** 13 minutes
EGG-FREE, VEGETARIAN, 30 MINUTES OR LESS

This is my favorite way to introduce eggplant to the little ones. The peel can stay a bit crunchy even when cooked, so I peel the eggplant in stripes, then dice them. This way, less than half of the eggplant cubes will still have the peel attached. The kids can try both options and see which one they like better.

1 tablespoon sea salt, plus ½ teaspoon, divided

1 pound bowtie pasta

4 tablespoons extra-virgin olive oil, divided

2 eggplants, peeled in stripes and diced

2 heirloom tomatoes, diced

¼ cup crumbled feta cheese

¼ cup Taggiasca black olives, pitted and chopped

2 tablespoons pine nuts

1 tablespoon minced fresh thyme

1. Fill a large pot with water, add 1 tablespoon salt, and bring it to a boil over high heat. Cook the pasta according to the package instructions. Drain the pasta, reserving ½ cup of the pasta water.

2. In a large sauté pan or skillet over medium heat, warm 2 tablespoons olive oil for 1 minute. Add the eggplant, tomatoes, and the remaining ½ teaspoon salt and cook for 8 minutes, stirring occasionally.

3. In a large bowl, mix together the pasta and eggplant mixture. Add the feta, olives, pine nuts, and thyme. Stir to combine. If the sauce is too thick, stir in the pasta water 1 tablespoon at a time, until you reach the desired consistency.

4. To make it more toddler-friendly: Reserve some of the eggplant and tomato–coated pasta before you mix in the olives, feta, and pine nuts. Serve the pasta with a little bit of crumbled feta, one pine nut, and one olive on the side. It will expose them to the flavors without overwhelming them.

Prep help: This can also be made as a cold pasta salad, which works well in a lunch box or at a picnic. After cooking the pasta, drain it in a colander and run cold water over it. Let the pasta sit to cool completely and release any excess water. Add all the ingredients to the pasta and mix thoroughly.

BROCCOLI RISOTTO

Serves 4 | **Prep time:** 10 minutes / **Cook time:** 25 minutes
EGG-FREE, GLUTEN-FREE, NUT-FREE, VEGETARIAN, ONE-POT

Most people cook risotto on the weekend or for a special occasion, but once you see how easy it is to prepare, you'll add it to your weeknight meal plan. Its creaminess and cheesy flavor will conquer any toddler's pickiness.

3 tablespoons extra-virgin olive oil

½ white onion, minced

3 cups broccoli florets, chopped into small pieces

3 cups vegetable broth

1 cup Arborio or carnaroli rice

1 tablespoon plain Greek yogurt

1 cup grated Parmesan cheese

1. In a large pot over medium heat, warm the olive oil. Add the onion and cook until golden, about 3 minutes. Add the broccoli and cook, stirring frequently, for 4 minutes.

2. **To make it more toddler-friendly:** Pulse the broccoli in a food processor before adding to the pot.

3. In a small saucepan over medium-low heat, warm the vegetable broth.

4. Add the rice to the pot with the broccoli and stir. Set a timer for 18 minutes. Let the rice toast, stirring frequently, until it gets shiny, about 3 minutes. Add 3 ladles of broth, stir, and let simmer until almost all the liquid is absorbed by the rice.

5. Add another ladle of broth, stir, and let simmer until the liquid is absorbed. Continue adding broth, one ladle at a time, and wait for the liquid to be absorbed before adding another.

6. When the timer goes off, remove the pan from the heat, add the Greek yogurt and the Parmesan cheese, and stir to combine. Serve warm, or cooled to room temperature for toddlers.

Swap it! You don't have broccoli in the refrigerator? No problem, chop up some zucchini, asparagus, green beans, kale, or add sweet peas. For something a bit sweeter, try pumpkin or butternut squash.

BAKED SPINACH PASTA CASSEROLE

Serves 6 | **Prep time:** 15 minutes / **Cook time:** 20 minutes
EGG-FREE, VEGETARIAN

Baked pasta is such a comfort food both for toddlers and adults. If your little ones don't like anything green, this recipe might change their minds. The spinach and the ricotta create a lovely cheesy cream that is so tasty that the color will be forgotten.

1 tablespoon sea salt,
    plus ½ teaspoon, divided
1 pound elbow pasta
2 tablespoons extra-virgin
    olive oil
½ medium yellow
    onion, minced
2 garlic cloves, minced
16 ounces fresh spinach
5 tablespoons
    ricotta cheese
1 tablespoon hemp seeds
½ teaspoon
    ground nutmeg
½ cup grated
    Parmesan cheese
3 tablespoons almond meal

1. Fill a large pot with water, add 1 tablespoon of salt and the pasta, and bring to a boil. Cook for 4 minutes less time than the package directions. Drain the pasta, reserving ½ cup of the pasta water.

2. In a large skillet over medium heat, warm the olive oil for 1 minute. Add the onion and garlic and cook for 2 minutes. Add the spinach and remaining ½ teaspoon of salt, stir, and cook for 4 minutes. Transfer to a large bowl and let cool. Mix in the ricotta, hemp seeds, and nutmeg.

3. To make it more toddler-friendly: In a food processor, process the spinach, ricotta, hemp seeds, and nutmeg until completely smooth. Transfer to a large bowl.

4. Add the pasta to the ricotta-spinach mixture and stir to combine. Stir in the reserved pasta water to prevent the casserole from drying out while baking. Transfer the pasta mixture to a baking dish.

5. Preheat the oven to broil.

6. In a small bowl, mix together the Parmesan cheese and almond meal. Sprinkle the mixture over the top of the pasta and broil for 10 minutes, until the cheese melts and starts to brown. Serve warm, or cooled to room temperature for toddlers.

Swap it! If you are looking for a gluten-free option that satisfies toddlers and adults, I suggest purchasing rice pasta or a rice and quinoa blend. I also tested pasta made with corn flour and that works, too. All three will maintain their shape while baking. If you want a super soft texture, use a lentil- or bean-flour pasta.

Fish Grain Bowl, page 92

5

FISH STICK–FREE SEAFOOD MEALS

You might be surprised, but I consider fish one of the most toddler-friendly foods. From a nutritional point of view, fish provides a lean, high-quality protein, minerals, vitamins D and B, and omega-3 fatty acids that are essential for your kids' brain and nervous system development. Salmon, tuna, tilapia, shrimp, sole, cod, mahi-mahi, trout, catfish, crab, pollock, and whitefish are all excellent choices because they all have a delicate flavor and great texture that will appeal to toddlers. Fish is also really easy (and fast!) to cook. Give these recipes a try; they'll get your toddler "hooked" on fish . . . along with the whole family.

Shrimp and Avocado Salad 80

Tuna Panzanella 81

Cauliflower and Fish Croquettes 82

Salmon and Broccoli Fusilli 83

Cod and Zucchini Shells Pasta 84

Skillet Mahi-Mahi with Pesto, Tomatoes, and Olives 85

Baked Salmon with Asparagus and Mushrooms 86

Shrimp-Stuffed Zucchini Boats 87

Sole and Bulgur–Stuffed Tomatoes 88

Salmon and Zucchini Skewers 91

Fish Grain Bowl 92

Sheet Pan Tilapia with Potatoes, Tomatoes, and Olives 94

SHRIMP AND AVOCADO SALAD

Serves 4 | **Prep time:** 10 minutes / **Cook time:** 6 minutes
DAIRY-FREE, EGG-FREE, GLUTEN-FREE, NUT-FREE, 30 MINUTES OR LESS

Avocado is definitely a super food that kids love. It's a win-win situation for parents and kids: healthy omega-3 fatty acids offered in a form they will actually eat. In combination with the shrimp, this recipe provides needed protein and you can feel confident that you are serving a healthy and complete meal for the whole family.

3 tablespoons extra-virgin
   olive oil
2 garlic cloves, minced
1 teaspoon minced
   fresh parsley
1 pound raw shrimp
½ teaspoon sweet paprika
Pinch sea salt
4 Hass avocados, peeled,
   pitted, and diced, shells
   reserved
½ cup frozen corn, thawed

1. In a medium skillet over medium-high heat, warm the olive oil. Add the garlic and parsley and cook for 2 minutes. Add the shrimp, paprika, and salt and cook until they turn pink, about 4 minutes. Be careful not to overcook them. Turn off the heat and let the shrimp cool.

2. Add the avocado and corn and stir to combine.

3. To make it more toddler-friendly: Cut the cooked shrimp into toddler-size bites and mash the avocado with a fork.

4. Spoon the salad into the avocado shells and serve.

Make it fun. Transform your avocado into a sailing boat simply by inserting half a *grissini* (an Italian breadstick) in the center and two pita bread triangles on the sides to look like a mast and sails.

TUNA PANZANELLA

Serves 6 | **Prep time:** 20 minutes

DAIRY-FREE, EGG-FREE, NUT-FREE, 30 MINUTES OR LESS

Panzanella is a southern Italian recipe made with bread and tomatoes. Feel free to add whatever else you like. Buy tuna canned in extra-virgin olive oil—it tastes the best. This salad is perfect for little palates, because the bread gets super soft and spongy and won't hurt tender toddler mouths. The bread needs time to dry out, so start this recipe the day before you plan to make it.

1½ baguettes, cut into 1-inch pieces

1½ cups quartered cherry tomatoes

5 tablespoons extra-virgin olive oil, divided

½ teaspoon sea salt

2 cups water

2 tablespoons apple cider vinegar

10 ounces canned tuna in extra-virgin olive oil

1 cup frozen corn, thawed

1 Hass avocado, peeled, pitted, and diced

1 Persian cucumber, diced

½ cup sweet green olives, pitted and minced

5 fresh basil leaves

2 tablespoons soy sauce

1 lemon, cut into quarters and very thinly sliced

1. The day before you want to serve the salad, place the baguette pieces in a large bowl and leave them on the kitchen counter to dry out.

2. In a medium bowl, mix together the tomatoes, 3 tablespoons olive oil, and the salt. Set aside.

3. In a measuring cup, mix together the water with the vinegar and pour it over the dried bread. Let sit for 5 minutes.

4. Add the tuna, corn, avocado, cucumber, olives, basil, soy sauce, lemon, and the remaining 2 tablespoons olive oil and mix until combined. Add the tomatoes, stir to combine, and serve.

5. To make it more toddler-friendly: Up the bread-to-stuff ratio by using 2 baguettes. What kid doesn't like bread?

Swap it! Your toddler doesn't like tuna? Make it using mozzarella instead. And if you can find *Mozzarella di Bufala* (a creamy version of the traditional), the result will be even better.

CAULIFLOWER AND FISH CROQUETTES

Serves 6 | **Prep time:** 15 minutes / **Cook time:** 30 minutes
DAIRY-FREE, GLUTEN-FREE

The cauliflower is such a game-changer in this recipe! It not only adds nutrients but also gives body and moisture to the croquettes. I prefer to bake them instead of pan frying for a lighter option. The almond meal coating gives a lovely nutty flavor.

1½ cups water

½ pound cauliflower,
  cut into pieces

1 pound catfish fillet,
  cut into big pieces

3 tablespoons almond
  meal, plus 1 cup
  for coating

1 tablespoon
  parsley, minced

1 teaspoon garlic powder

1 egg

½ teaspoon sea salt

¼ cup extra-virgin olive oil

1. In a large pot over medium-high heat, bring the water to a boil. Add the cauliflower, cover, then reduce the heat to medium-low. Cook until tender, 8 to 10 minutes.

2. Preheat the oven to 400°F. Line a baking sheet with parchment paper.

3. In a food processor, pulse the catfish for a few seconds until finely minced. Add the steamed cauliflower and pulse for a few seconds to combine the ingredients. Transfer to a large bowl and mix together with 3 tablespoons almond meal, the parsley, garlic, egg, and salt.

4. Using your hands, form small croquettes with 1 tablespoon of the mixture for each one. If the mixture is too sticky, wet your hands with water.

5. Pour 1 cup almond meal in a small bowl. Dredge each croquette in the almond meal, making sure to cover it all over.

6. Place the croquettes onto the prepared baking sheet and drizzle with the olive oil. Bake for 20 minutes, until heated through.

Make it fun. Make the croquettes into any shape you like. An oval croquette can easily become a fish by narrowing one side. Add a slice of olive to create an eye. Ask your toddler to help you decorate them.

SALMON AND BROCCOLI FUSILLI

Serves 6 | **Prep time:** 15 minutes / **Cook time:** 13 minutes

EGG-FREE, NUT-FREE, 30 MINUTES OR LESS

I try to serve salmon to my kids at least once a week: It's high in the good fats that help the brain develop and it's low in mercury. For anyone bored after eating too much plain roasted salmon or for kids suspicious of any kind of fish, this dish will set them straight.

1 pound fusilli pasta

3 tablespoons extra-virgin olive oil, divided

½ medium white onion, minced

4 garlic cloves, minced

1 head broccoli, stems discarded, florets cut into small pieces

¼ cup warm water

Pinch sea salt

8 ounces salmon, diced

1 tablespoon minced fresh parsley

3 tablespoons plain yogurt

1. Bring a large pot of water to a boil, add the pasta, and cook according to the package instructions. Drain the pasta, reserving 1 cup of the pasta water. Set aside.

2. In a large sauté pan or skillet over medium-high heat, warm 2 tablespoons olive oil. Add the onion and garlic and cook for 3 minutes. Reduce the heat to medium-low, add the broccoli florets, parsley, warm water, and salt and cook for 8 minutes. Transfer the broccoli to a bowl and set aside.

3. To make it more toddler-friendly: Process the cooked broccoli in a food processor until smooth and set aside.

4. In the same skillet over medium heat, add the remaining 1 tablespoon olive oil, the salmon, and salt and cook for 2 minutes, stirring occasionally.

5. Add the broccoli back to the skillet and stir. Remove from the heat.

6. Add the pasta and yogurt to the salmon mixture and stir to combine. If the sauce is too thick, add the reserved pasta water, 1 tablespoon at a time, until you reach the desired consistency. Serve warm, or cooled to room temperature for toddlers.

Swap it! If you are looking for a grain-free, gluten-free recipe, use a pasta made with rice and quinoa, which is softer and creamier. Your toddler might like it even more.

COD AND ZUCCHINI SHELLS PASTA

Serves 4 | **Prep time:** 20 minutes / **Cook time:** 20 minutes
DAIRY-FREE, EGG-FREE

Seafood and vegetables are always a great combo, but when combined with pasta, they make an amazing complete meal for the whole family. All the ingredients are chopped into bite-size pieces, which lets the cod and zucchini sauce naturally fill the pasta shells, giving you the perfect bite from start to finish. I've included anchovies, which substitute for salt while providing extra omega-3 fatty acids to feed your toddler's brain development.

1 pound shell pasta or any
   short pasta
1 tablespoon sea salt
4 tablespoons extra-virgin
   olive oil, divided
2 anchovy fillets or
   ½ teaspoon sea salt
2 garlic cloves, minced
2 zucchinis, quartered and
   cut into thick slices
1 heirloom tomato, seeds
   removed and diced
½ pound cod, diced
1 tablespoon minced
   fresh parsley
2 tablespoons almond meal
2 tablespoons
   breadcrumbs
Parmesan cheese,
   for serving

1. Bring a pot of water to a boil over high heat, add the pasta and salt, and cook according to the package instructions. Drain the pasta, reserving 1 cup of the pasta water. Set aside.

2. In a large sauté pan or skillet over medium heat, warm 2 tablespoons olive oil. Add the anchovies and garlic and cook for 2 minutes. Add the zucchinis and cook for an additional 4 minutes. Add the tomatoes, cod, and parsley, then stir and cook for 5 minutes. Transfer the mixture to a large bowl and set aside.

3. In the same skillet over medium heat, stir together the almond meal and breadcrumbs until they start to brown, about 2 minutes.

4. Add the pasta to the large bowl with the cod and stir to combine. Add the breadcrumb mixture and the remaining 2 tablespoons olive oil and stir gently to combine. Serve warm.

5. **To make it more toddler-friendly:** Cool to room temperature and add a generous handful of grated Parmesan cheese on top.

Swap it! Can't find cod? Use whatever fish you can find that is freshest, such as catfish, pollock, or halibut.

SKILLET MAHI-MAHI WITH PESTO, TOMATOES, AND OLIVES

Serves 4 | **Prep time:** 20 minutes / **Cook time:** 10 minutes
EGG-FREE, GLUTEN-FREE, ONE-POT, 30 MINUTES OR LESS, 5 INGREDIENTS OR LESS

I used to prepare this aromatic basil pesto–infused recipe using chicken. Then, one day I ran out of chicken and tried it with mahi-mahi. To my surprise, it was even better with fish! It was way more tender and so delicious. Now my kids call it "the green fish."

1 pound mahi-mahi,
   cut into 1-inch pieces
¼ cup basil pesto
2 tablespoons extra-virgin
   olive oil
1 cup chopped cherry
   tomatoes
¼ cup pitted and
   quartered Taggiasca
   black olives
Pinch sea salt
4 fresh basil
   leaves, chopped

1. In a large bowl, gently mix together the mahi-mahi and pesto, cover, and marinate in the refrigerator for at least 20 minutes.

2. In a large nonstick sauté pan or skillet over medium heat, warm the olive oil for 30 seconds. Add the marinated mahi-mahi, tomatoes, and salt. Cook, stirring occasionally, for 4 minutes. Add the olives and continue to cook, stirring occasionally, until the fish is cooked through, about 6 minutes. Remove from the heat and stir in the basil. Serve warm.

3. **To make it more toddler-friendly:** Cool to room temperature and skip the olives and fresh basil. Save them to garnish the top of the adult portions only.

Prep help: To save time, you can marinate the fish with the pesto overnight. The longer it marinates, the deeper the flavor of the pesto will penetrate into the fish.

BAKED SALMON WITH ASPARAGUS AND MUSHROOMS

Serves 4 | **Prep time:** 10 minutes / **Cook time:** 20 minutes

DAIRY-FREE, EGG-FREE, GLUTEN-FREE, NUT-FREE, ONE-POT, 30 MINUTES OR LESS

This recipe is a real lifesaver for hectic weeknights when you don't have time for anything. With only 10 minutes of prep time, you can prepare a gourmet-style meal that will impress your family and everyone will eat it. Salmon is a healthy option for little ones, but the flavor can be a bit too intense for them. When you bake it with this honey-Dijon sauce, you'll find that your toddler will love it.

1 (3-pound) salmon fillet

1 pound
   asparagus, trimmed

1 cup sliced cremini
   mushrooms

5 tablespoons extra-virgin
   olive oil

3 tablespoons
   Dijon mustard

Juice of ½ lemon

1 tablespoon honey

½ teaspoon sea salt

4 garlic cloves, minced

1. Preheat the oven to 400°F. Line a baking sheet with parchment paper.

2. Pat the salmon dry with a paper towel and place it in the center of the prepared baking sheet. Place the asparagus and mushrooms on each side of the salmon.

3. To make it more toddler-friendly: Cut the asparagus into ½-inch pieces. It will be more tender and easier for kids to eat.

4. In a small bowl, whisk together the olive oil, mustard, lemon juice, honey, salt, and garlic. Pour the sauce over the salmon and drizzle it over the asparagus and mushrooms.

5. Bake for 15 minutes, then set the oven to broil and broil for 5 more minutes. Serve warm, or cooled to room temperature for toddlers.

Swap it! If asparagus is hard to find, use other seasonal vegetables, such as carrots, green beans, broccoli, zucchini, or fennel.

SHRIMP-STUFFED ZUCCHINI BOATS

Serves 4 | **Prep time:** 15 minutes / **Cook time:** 35 minutes
DAIRY-FREE, EGG-FREE, NUT-FREE

Kids will always love zucchini boats. After you fill each one with the shrimp stuffing, you can add a sail using a toothpick and a basil leaf. After your little one eats the insides, you can cut up the "boat" and let them eat that, too.

6 zucchinis

3 tablespoons extra-virgin
   olive oil

1 garlic clove, minced

Pinch sea salt

½ pound frozen cooked
   shrimp, thawed
   and chopped into
   small pieces

½ cup breadcrumbs

2 fresh mint leaves, minced

1 teaspoon minced
   fresh parsley

1. Preheat the oven to 400°F. Line a baking sheet with parchment paper.

2. Cut 4 of the zucchinis in half lengthwise. Using a teaspoon, scoop out the inner pulp, place it in a bowl, and set it aside. Place the zucchini shells on the prepared baking sheet and bake for 15 minutes. Let cool on the baking sheet.

3. Chop the remaining 2 zucchinis into small pieces.

4. In a large sauté pan or skillet over medium heat, warm the olive oil, add the garlic, and cook for 1 minute. Add the chopped zucchini, the reserved zucchini pulp, and the salt and cook for 6 minutes. Remove from the heat, add the shrimp, breadcrumbs, mint, and parsley and mix to combine.

5. Fill the zucchini boats with the shrimp mixture and bake for another 15 minutes. Serve 2 boats to each person.

If all else fails . . . You might be surprised, but if your little one doesn't want to eat these boats, you might change their mind by adding diced mango to the shrimp mixture. It will add a nice sweetness to the dish that many kids really like.

SOLE AND BULGUR-STUFFED TOMATOES

Serves 4 | **Prep time:** 15 minutes / **Cook time:** 40 minutes
DAIRY-FREE, EGG-FREE, NUT-FREE, 5 INGREDIENTS OR LESS

Baked tomatoes stuffed with a mixture of wheat bulgur and sole makes a filling, healthy meal. Serve it with the tomato lid on top and your kids can discover for themselves what's inside. Use two capers on the top part of the filling to turn it into a stuffed tomato with eyes. The bulgur can be prepared ahead and stored in the refrigerator, which will save you a few minutes.

½ cup bulgur

1 teaspoon sea salt, divided, plus more for seasoning

¾ cup water

4 heirloom tomatoes

4 sole fillets

1 garlic clove, minced

1 tablespoon minced fresh parsley

3 tablespoons extra-virgin olive oil

1. Preheat the oven to 400°F. Line a baking sheet with parchment paper.

2. In a medium saucepan over medium-high heat, mix together the bulgur, ½ teaspoon salt, and the water, and bring to a boil. Reduce the heat to medium-low and simmer, covered, until tender, about 12 minutes. Remove from the heat and let sit, covered, for 10 minutes. Fluff with a fork.

3. Cut off the top of each tomato to create a lid and set them aside. Using a spoon, scoop out the seeds and pulp.

4. Put the tomato pulp in a food processor and pulse several times to chop it. Squeeze out any extra liquid and put the tomato pulp in a bowl.

5. Place the sole fillets in the food processor and pulse a few times to chop them. Transfer the sole to the bowl with the tomatoes.

6. **To make it more toddler-friendly:** Pulse the sole fillets until they become a thick paste before transferring them to the bowl with the tomatoes.

7. Add the bulgur, garlic, parsley, and remaining ½ teaspoon salt to the bowl with the sole and tomatoes and stir to combine.

8. Place the hollowed-out tomatoes on the prepared baking sheet and sprinkle the insides with salt. Fill each tomato with the sole mix. Drizzle the olive oil over the top and cover with the tomato lids.

9. Bake for 25 to 30 minutes, until cooked through. Serve warm, or cooled to room temperature for toddlers.

Swap it! Don't have bulgur in the pantry? Don't worry: You can use couscous, rice, barley, or orzo, which are great substitutes.

SALMON AND ZUCCHINI SKEWERS

Serves 4 | **Prep time:** 10 minutes / **Cook time:** 10 minutes
DAIRY-FREE, EGG-FREE, GLUTEN-FREE, NUT-FREE, 30 MINUTES OR LESS

You don't need barbecue skills to make this recipe. These skewers can be cooked on the stove, too. For added flavor, marinate the zucchini with the salmon. Do you like your meals with lots of color? Alternate the zucchini with bell peppers, tomatoes, and red onions.

½ cup extra-virgin olive oil

¼ cup lemon juice

Zest of 1 lemon

8 garlic cloves, minced

2 tablespoons minced fresh dill

1 tablespoon honey

1½ teaspoons sea salt

1 pound skinless salmon, cut into 1-inch pieces

2 zucchinis, cut into 1-inch slices

1. Have 6 skewers ready. For wood skewers, rinse them in water before using.

2. In a small bowl, mix together the olive oil, lemon juice, lemon zest, garlic, dill, honey, and salt. Add the salmon, mix together, and marinate for 5 minutes.

3. Place the salmon and zucchini onto the skewers, alternating between them.

4. Heat a large sauté pan or skillet over high heat for 1 minute. Add the skewers and cook for 3 to 4 minutes, flip, and continue to cook for another 3 minutes on the other side, until the salmon turns a pale pink.

5. For safety reasons, remove the salmon and zucchini from the skewers before serving them to kids. Serve 1 skewer for kids and 2 for adults.

Make it fun. To make it more fun, give the kids introductory chopsticks or child-safe food picks to pick up the food.

FISH GRAIN BOWL

Serves 6 | **Prep time:** 20 minutes / **Cook time:** 30 minutes
EGG-FREE, NUT-FREE

This bowl is loaded with flavor and all the needed nutrients; it's also dressed with a fresh cilantro-yogurt sauce. The Israeli couscous pearls are an easy toddler favorite and less messy than traditional couscous, which is much smaller.

2 medium sweet potatoes, peeled and diced

1 medium head of broccoli, chopped with stems discarded

5 tablespoons extra-virgin olive oil, plus ½ cup, divided

3 garlic cloves, minced, divided

1 teaspoon sea salt, divided, plus more for seasoning

½ pound halibut, diced

1 cup packed fresh cilantro

1 tablespoon plain Greek yogurt

2 teaspoons honey

Juice of ½ lemon

2 cups cooked Israeli couscous

1 cup shelled edamame

1 cup fresh baby spinach

2 scallions, chopped, for serving

1 tablespoon sesame seeds, for serving

1. Preheat the oven to 400°F. Line a baking sheet with parchment paper.

2. In a medium bowl, mix together the sweet potatoes, broccoli, 2 tablespoons olive oil, ⅓ of the minced garlic, and a pinch salt.

3. Transfer the mixture to the prepared baking sheet and roast for 20 minutes. Remove from the oven, but leave the oven on.

4. In a bowl, mix the halibut with 2 tablespoons olive oil, ⅓ of the minced garlic, and a pinch salt. Add the halibut to the baking sheet, return it to the oven, and bake for an additional 10 minutes.

5. In a food processor, process the cilantro, yogurt, ½ cup olive oil, honey, the remaining ½ teaspoon salt, and lemon juice until smooth. Set aside.

6. In a large bowl, gently mix together the Israeli couscous, edamame, baby spinach, roasted vegetables, and halibut. Serve in individual bowls with cilantro-yogurt dressing on top. For the adults, sprinkle the top with scallions and sesame seeds.

7. **To make it more toddler-friendly:** You can place the ingredients separately on a divided plate or even in a muffin tin, with the dressing on the side for kids who don't like their foods to touch each other. They can choose to mix and match any way they like.

Prep help: You can cut the recipe time in half by preparing some of the components ahead of time. Cook the Israeli couscous and the dressing the day before and store them in the refrigerator. Even the roasted veggies and halibut can be prepared in advance and reheated on the stove for 5 minutes before combining in the bowls. If all the components are already prepared, the bowls will be ready in 10 minutes.

SHEET PAN TILAPIA WITH POTATOES, TOMATOES, AND OLIVES

Serves 6 | **Prep time:** 20 minutes / **Cook time:** 25 minutes

EGG-FREE, ONE-POT

A super simple one-pot (or, one baking sheet) meal, this recipe is loaded with flavor and is easy to prepare. Tilapia is already a very toddler-friendly fish, but with the cheesy almond crust, your little ones will enjoy it even more.

6 medium russet potatoes, thinly sliced

2 pounds tilapia fillets

5 tablespoons extra-virgin olive oil, divided

¼ cup breadcrumbs

¼ cup grated Parmesan cheese

¼ cup almond meal

1 garlic clove, minced

1 tablespoon minced fresh parsley

½ teaspoon sea salt

1 cup cherry tomatoes

2 tablespoons pitted olives

4 ounces snow peas

1. Preheat the oven to 400°F. Line a baking sheet with parchment paper.

2. Place a layer of potatoes on the prepared baking sheet, placing them right next to each other. Place the tilapia fillets on top of the potatoes.

3. In a bowl, mix together 2 tablespoons olive oil, breadcrumbs, Parmesan cheese, almond meal, garlic, parsley, and salt. Sprinkle the tilapia with the breadcrumb mixture.

4. Place the cherry tomatoes and olives on top and the snow peas in between the fish fillets. Drizzle the remaining 3 tablespoons olive oil over the top.

5. Bake for 25 minutes, until cooked through.

6. To make it more toddler-friendly: Blend some of the potatoes, roasted cherry tomatoes, and olives together to make a "sauce" for the fish and snow peas. Add a few tablespoons of the cooking liquid from the baking sheet to thin the sauce and enhance the flavors.

If all else fails . . . Pasta always comes to the rescue. Cook a handful of elbow pasta in a small saucepan according to the package instructions and combine the pasta with a small portion of the baked tilapia and snow peas, tossed in the "sauce" you made from blending the potatoes, tomatoes, and olives.

Bowties with Chicken and Peas, page 106

6

NON-NUGGET CHICKEN DINNERS

Chicken is definitely high on the list of toddlers' favorite foods—the flavor is mild, there are no crazy colors, and the texture is appealing. But chicken can go way beyond chicken nuggets (and even for nuggets, I think the best ones are homemade; they are super easy to prepare and loaded with flavor). Here you'll find my family favorites featuring chicken. From pasta dishes to casseroles, skewers to roll-ups, each recipe is easy to prepare and can be changed by substituting other ingredients if your kids object to one.

Roasted Chicken and Vegetable Quinoa Salad 98

Chicken Soup for a Cold 100

Pesto Chicken Pinwheels 102

Quinoa Chicken Bites 103

Chicken and Broccoli Meatballs in Tomato Sauce 104

Bowties with Chicken and Peas 106

Baked Chicken, Ham, and Mozzarella Rolls 107

Turkey Sausage and Zucchini Roll-Ups 108

Skillet Turkey and Peppers 109

Baked Curried Chicken and Vegetable Rice 111

The Easiest Roast Chicken Ever 112

Creamy Coconut and Turmeric Turkey 113

ROASTED CHICKEN AND VEGETABLE QUINOA SALAD

Serves 6 | **Prep time:** 15 minutes / **Cook time:** 30 minutes

DAIRY-FREE, EGG-FREE, GLUTEN-FREE, NUT-FREE, ONE-POT

Roasting the chicken with the vegetables makes the difference here: The sugars in the vegetables are caramelized by the heat, which enhances their flavor. The tenderness of the vegetables makes them very easy to eat for young children. Cook up some quinoa on the weekend and store it in the refrigerator, and recipes like this will come together very quickly on weeknights.

1 (10-ounce) whole chicken breast, cut in half

4 tablespoons extra-virgin olive oil, divided

½ teaspoon sea salt, divided

1 broccoli head, cut into florets and stems discarded

1 large carrot, peeled and chopped

1 Roma tomato, diced

2 fresh rosemary sprigs

2 garlic cloves, peeled and cut in half

2 cups cooked red quinoa

1. Preheat the oven to 425°F. Line a baking sheet with parchment paper. Have the cooked quinoa ready in a large bowl.

2. Place the chicken breast halves on the prepared baking sheet, brush with 1 tablespoon olive oil, and sprinkle with ¼ teaspoon salt.

3. Place the broccoli, carrots, tomatoes, rosemary, and garlic around the chicken. Drizzle with the remaining 3 tablespoons olive oil and sprinkle with the remaining ¼ teaspoon salt.

4. Roast for 20 to 30 minutes, until the chicken reaches an internal temperature of 165°F and the vegetables are nicely roasted.

5. Cover the baking sheet with parchment paper and let rest on a wire rack for 10 minutes to let the juices set in the chicken. Discard the rosemary.

6. **To make it more toddler-friendly:** Cut the chicken and the vegetables into smaller, toddler-size pieces.

7. Add the chicken and vegetables to the quinoa and stir to combine. Serve warm, or cooled to room temperature for toddlers.

If all else fails . . . Some toddlers do not like the concept of salads. They object to having several ingredients mixed together. That's when a deconstructed approach can help. For this recipe, place the chicken, vegetables, and quinoa on a plate, making sure to put them in separate piles. For extra flavor, top the quinoa with 1 tablespoon grated Parmesan cheese. You'd be surprised how presenting food in a different way like this will get a different reaction.

CHICKEN SOUP FOR A COLD

Serves 4 | **Prep time:** 15 minutes / **Cook time:** 3 hours / **Chill time:** 30 minutes
EGG-FREE, NUT-FREE, ONE-POT, FREEZER-FRIENDLY

Grandma's remedies are always the best, and chicken soup is one of my favorites. Healing, comforting, and easy to prepare, this soup is warm, nutritious, and helps relieve the symptoms of the common cold. This chicken soup uses about half of the broth. Freeze the remaining broth for up to 3 months, and all you'll need to do when you want to make this soup again is defrost the broth, add the vegetables, and cook for 30 minutes.

For the Broth

- 3 pounds bony chicken pieces (legs, wings, neck, and back bones)
- 2 medium carrots, peeled and roughly chopped
- 2 celery stalks, roughly chopped
- 1 small parsnip, peeled and roughly chopped
- 1 medium yellow onion, peeled and cut in quarters
- 4 garlic cloves, peeled
- 1 tablespoon dried thyme
- 3 bay leaves
- 1½ teaspoons sea salt
- 8 cups cold water

To Make the Broth

1. In a large pot over medium-high heat, mix together the chicken pieces, carrots, celery, parsnip, onion, garlic, thyme, bay leaves, salt, and cold water and bring to a boil. Reduce the heat to medium-low and simmer, uncovered, for 2½ hours. Remove from the heat and let cool for 30 minutes.

2. Set a colander over a large bowl and strain the broth, discarding the solids. Set aside 4 cups of broth for the soup and freeze the remainder in airtight containers for up to 3 months.

For the Soup

1 medium carrot, peeled, quartered, then cut into small pieces

1 small zucchini, quartered and cut into small pieces

1 celery stalk, thinly sliced

¾ cup small-size pasta

½ teaspoon sea salt

¼ cup grated Parmesan cheese, for serving

To Prepare the Soup

1. Pour the reserved broth back into the large pot, add the carrot, zucchini, and celery and cook over medium heat for 15 minutes. Add the pasta and salt and cook for 8 minutes, or follow the instructions on the package.

2. Serve with a generous handful of Parmesan cheese on top.

If all else fails . . . When your little one is under the weather, they can be pickier than usual, so the easier the recipe, the better. Serve the chicken broth with only pasta and Parmesan. All the good nutrients will come from the broth and will help your toddler get some relief from their cold symptoms.

PESTO CHICKEN PINWHEELS

Serves 4 | **Prep time:** 15 minutes / **Cook time:** 30 minutes
EGG-FREE, GLUTEN-FREE, ONE-POT

You can't really go wrong with these roll-ups. They are easy to prepare, fun to look at, and they taste great, so this one gets a big toddler thumbs-up!

1½ whole chicken breasts

⅔ cup basil pesto

5 ounces sliced
   Gouda cheese

2 tablespoons extra-virgin
   olive oil

2 carrots, peeled and cut
   into thick slices

2 zucchinis, quartered
   lengthwise and
   thickly sliced

½ teaspoon sea salt

½ cup vegetable broth

1. Cut the chicken breasts horizontally into large, very thin slices. Pound them with a kitchen mallet to make them all the same thickness.

2. Place 1 teaspoon pesto and 1 slice of cheese on each piece of chicken. Roll up each piece and secure it with 1 or 2 toothpicks.

3. In a large skillet over medium-high heat, warm the olive oil. Add the chicken rolls and sear for 5 minutes, turning the rolls to cook them evenly.

4. Reduce the heat to medium-low and add the carrots, zucchini, salt, and broth. Cook for another 20 to 25 minutes, turning the rolls occasionally. Remove the toothpicks and serve warm, or cooled to room temperature for toddlers.

5. To make it more toddler-friendly: Cut the chicken rolls into slices and fan them out on a plate. Little ones will love their plate of pinwheels.

   Swap it! If you don't have pesto on hand, you can substitute tomato paste and transform the pesto pinwheels into pizza pinwheels.

QUINOA CHICKEN BITES

Serves 4 | **Prep time:** 15 minutes / **Cook time:** 10 minutes
GLUTEN-FREE, NUT-FREE, 30 MINUTES OR LESS

Forget about chicken nuggets, these cheesy, crunchy bites of tender chicken breast are a great dinner idea for toddlers . . . and adults, too. I like coating the outside with quinoa. Kids tend to like it, and it adds an extra punch of protein.

2 medium eggs

3 tablespoons grated
  Parmesan cheese

1 teaspoon minced
  fresh parsley

½ teaspoon sea salt

½ teaspoon ground
  turmeric

2 cups cooked quinoa

1 whole chicken breast,
  cut in small strips

6 tablespoons extra-virgin
  olive oil

1. In a large bowl, beat the eggs. Add the Parmesan cheese, parsley, salt, and turmeric and whisk well.

2. Put the cooked quinoa in a shallow bowl.

3. Coat 1 piece of chicken in the egg mixture, dredge it in the quinoa, making sure to coat all sides, and place on a large plate. Repeat with the rest of the chicken.

4. Line a plate with paper towels.

5. In a large skillet over medium heat, warm the oil for 1 minute. Add the chicken strips, leaving a little space between them and cook for 4 minutes. Flip them and continue to cook for another 4 minutes, until golden brown. Transfer to the paper towel–lined plate to absorb any extra oil. Serve warm, or cooled to room temperature for toddlers.

Swap it! If you have a bit more time, you can bake the chicken bites instead of pan frying them. Preheat the oven to 400°F. Line a baking sheet with parchment paper and drizzle some olive oil over the paper. Place the strips on the prepared baking sheet and bake for 25 minutes, flipping the chicken halfway through the baking time.

CHICKEN AND BROCCOLI MEATBALLS IN TOMATO SAUCE

Serves 6 | **Prep time:** 20 minutes / **Cook time:** 30 minutes

EGG-FREE, NUT-FREE, FREEZER-FRIENDLY

Thanks to the broccoli, these chicken meatballs are super moist and loaded with nutrients. The chia seeds act as a binder for the meatballs while also delivering extra omega-3 fatty acids. For a gluten-free option, use almond meal instead of breadcrumbs. The meatballs will have the same texture and an added nutty flavor.

2 cups water, divided

1 head broccoli, cut into florets, roughly chopped, and stems discarded

1 pound ground chicken

1½ cups breadcrumbs, divided

2 tablespoons chia seeds

2 tablespoons hemp seeds

3 tablespoons grated Parmesan cheese

1 teaspoon garlic powder

1 teaspoon dried thyme

Pinch sea salt

2 tablespoons extra-virgin olive oil

2 cups tomato sauce

1. In a large pot, bring about 1½ cups water to a boil over high heat. Add the broccoli, reduce the heat to medium, and steam until tender, about 8 minutes. Transfer the broccoli to a large bowl and mash with a fork.

2. To make it more toddler-friendly: Process the broccoli in a food processor for 30 seconds instead of mashing with a fork. The chicken balls will have a smoother consistency.

3. Add the ground chicken, ½ cup breadcrumbs, chia seeds, hemp seeds, Parmesan cheese, garlic powder, thyme, and salt and stir to combine.

4. In a shallow bowl, pour in the remaining 1 cup breadcrumbs.

5. Using your hands, take 1 tablespoon of the mixture, form it into a ball, roll it in the breadcrumbs, and place on a plate. Repeat with the remaining mixture.

6. To make it more toddler-friendly: Make the meatballs even smaller, using ½ tablespoon of the mixture. It does take a bit more time, but they will cook faster.

7. In a large skillet over medium heat, warm the olive oil for 30 seconds. Add the meatballs, making sure to leave some space between them. Brown the meatballs for 5 minutes, turning occasionally.

8. Add the tomato sauce and remaining ½ cup water, reduce the heat to medium-low, and cook until the meatballs are cooked through, stirring occasionally, about 15 minutes. Serve warm, or cooled to room temperature for toddlers.

9. Store in an airtight container in the refrigerator for up to 2 days, or freeze for up to 3 months.

Prep help: Make a double batch of meatballs, cook them in the skillet, and freeze half of them in an airtight container for up to 3 months. Cook the rest of the meatballs with the tomato sauce to eat right away. You can use the meatballs straight from the freezer: Start from step 8 and cook them with the tomato sauce until heated through. I don't know how many times these frozen meatballs have saved me at dinnertime.

BOWTIES WITH CHICKEN AND PEAS

Serves 4 | **Prep time:** 10 minutes / **Cook time:** 20 minutes
EGG-FREE, NUT-FREE, 30 MINUTES OR LESS

Pasta, chicken, veggies, and legumes: an easy and nutritionally complete meal that can be prepared in no time for a weeknight dinner. When pasta is involved, the kids are usually very happy. Feel free to have fun with novelty pasta shapes: Alphabet pasta is definitely a super fun option.

1 pound bowtie pasta

1 tablespoon sea salt, plus ½ teaspoon, divided

3 tablespoons extra-virgin olive oil

½ whole chicken breast, diced

12 cherry tomatoes, cut in quarters

1 leek, halved lengthwise and thinly sliced

1 cup frozen sweet peas

½ white onion, minced

1 tablespoon minced fresh parsley, for serving

¼ cup grated Parmesan cheese, for serving

1. Bring a large pot of water to a boil over high heat. Add the pasta and 1 tablespoon salt and cook according to the package instructions. Drain the pasta, reserving 1 cup of the pasta water.

2. In a large skillet over medium heat, warm the olive oil for 1 minute. Add the chicken and cook, stirring often, for 6 minutes. Season with the remaining ½ teaspoon salt.

3. To make it more toddler-friendly: Use ground chicken instead of diced chicken and the sauce will be more like a Bolognese.

4. Add the tomatoes, leek, peas, and onion and cook for 8 minutes.

5. Add the pasta to the chicken sauce and stir to combine. If the sauce is too thick, add the pasta water, 1 tablespoon at a time, until it reaches your desired consistency.

6. Serve warm, or cooled to room temperature for toddlers, with parsley and a handful of Parmesan cheese on top.

Swap it! For a greater combination of flavors that's great for fall or winter, swap out the leek, tomato, and sweet peas and replace with 1 cup chopped mushrooms, 1 cup chopped broccoli florets, and ½ cup pumpkin cut into ½-inch cubes.

BAKED CHICKEN, HAM, AND MOZZARELLA ROLLS

Serves 6 | **Prep time:** 20 minutes / **Cook time:** 30 minutes
EGG-FREE, GLUTEN-FREE, ONE-POT

The carrots in this recipe are thinly sliced in long curls, so they'll cook faster in the oven and are easily handled by toddlers. To make this recipe even more fun, you can use rainbow carrots, so you'll end up with a multi-colored pile of yellow, orange, and purple spirals that the kids will love. If you want to make these roll-ups more substantial, steam 2 cups fresh spinach, squeeze out the liquid, chop finely, place 1 tablespoon on each chicken slice along with the other ingredients, and roll up the chicken. You'll need toothpicks to hold the chicken rolls together.

4 tablespoons extra-virgin
   olive oil, divided
1 whole boneless, skinless
   chicken breast, cut in half
4 slices ham, each
   cut in half
8 ounces mozzarella, cut
   into 8 thin slices
8 fresh sage leaves
4 carrots, peeled and thinly
   sliced lengthwise with a
   vegetable peeler
Pinch sea salt
2 tablespoons pine nuts

1. Preheat the oven to 425°F. Grease a baking pan with 1 tablespoon olive oil. Have 8 to 10 toothpicks ready.

2. Cut each piece of chicken into 4 slices. Place each slice in between 2 pieces of plastic wrap or parchment paper and pound with a kitchen mallet or rolling pin until it is ¼-inch thick.

3. Place 1 piece of ham, 1 slice of mozzarella, and 1 sage leaf on top of each piece of chicken. Roll up each piece of chicken and seal with a water soaked toothpick. You might need more than one toothpick for large slices.

4. Place the chicken rolls into the prepared baking pan.

5. Arrange the carrots around the chicken rolls, sprinkle with salt, and drizzle with the remaining 3 tablespoons olive oil.

6. Bake for 20 minutes. Add the pine nuts and continue baking for 5 to 10 minutes, until the chicken rolls are cooked through and are golden.

7. To make it toddler-friendly: Remove the toothpicks from the chicken rolls, cut them into slices, and fan them out onto a plate.

Swap it! For a stronger flavor, use Pecorino or aged Manchego instead of mozzarella cheese.

TURKEY SAUSAGE AND ZUCCHINI ROLL-UPS

Serves 4 | **Prep time:** 10 minutes / **Cook time:** 15 minutes
EGG-FREE, GLUTEN-FREE, NUT-FREE, 30 MINUTES OR LESS

Beware, these cheesy sausage zucchini bites can be addictive! When my kids were smaller, I would take the skewers out of the rolls and put them on a plate and pretend they were snails. Then I would tell them a story of the little snails that wanted to fly. Try creating some stories of your own. They go a long way when trying to make dinnertime more fun.

2 zucchinis, cut lengthwise
into 6 (⅛-inch-thick) slices

3 turkey sausages

3 tablespoons
cream cheese

1 yellow bell pepper, cut
into 1-inch squares

6 cherry tomatoes,
cut in half

3 tablespoons extra-virgin
olive oil

Pinch sea salt

1 cup vegetable broth

6 fresh sage leaves

1. Have 6 skewers ready. For wood skewers, rinse them in water before using.

2. Place the zucchini slices on a microwave-safe plate and microwave for 1 minute until they are soft enough to roll without breaking. Set aside.

3. In a food processor, pulse the turkey sausage and cream cheese until smooth.

4. On a clean work surface, lay out the zucchini slices and spread each one with the sausage mixture. Gently roll up each slice. Place a zucchini roll on a skewer, followed by bell pepper, tomato, another zucchini roll, bell pepper, and tomato. Repeat with the rest of the skewers.

5. In a large sauté pan or skillet over medium-high heat, warm the olive oil. Place the skewers in the skillet, sprinkle with salt, and cook until they are browned, about 5 minutes, turning to cook on all sides.

6. Add the broth and sage, reduce the heat to medium-low, cover, and cook until cooked through, about 10 minutes, turning the skewers a few times. Serve warm, or cooled to room temperature for toddlers.

Prep help: This recipe takes less than 30 minutes to prepare but if you end up making more zucchini roll-ups than needed, freeze the extra ones before cooking them. When you are ready to enjoy, place the frozen roll-ups directly in the skillet and cook them for 15 minutes before serving.

SKILLET TURKEY AND PEPPERS

Serves 4 | **Prep time:** 10 minutes / **Cook time:** 20 to 25 minutes

DAIRY-FREE, EGG-FREE, GLUTEN-FREE, NUT-FREE, ONE-POT

I love the bright fall colors in this family-friendly recipe. What really captures the kids' attention are the shapes of the vegetables and turkey. Everything is cut in thin strips, and when it's all cooked, each serving looks a little like a plate of noodles.

5 tablespoons extra-virgin
  olive oil

½ yellow onion, minced

2 red bell peppers, seeded
  and cut into thin strips

2 yellow bell peppers,
  seeded and cut into
  thin strips

Pinch sea salt

1 pound turkey breast, cut
  into thin strips

15 cherry tomatoes, cut in
  half, seeds removed

½ cup chicken broth

1 tablespoon minced
  fresh parsley

1. In a large sauté pan or skillet over medium heat, warm the olive oil. Add the onion and cook for 5 minutes. Add the red and yellow bell peppers and cook for 8 to 9 minutes. Season with salt.

2. Add the turkey, tomatoes, and broth, then reduce the heat to medium-low and simmer for 8 to 10 minutes, until the turkey is cooked through. Remove from the heat and add the parsley. Serve warm, or cooled to room temperature for toddlers.

If all else fails . . . Your kid isn't fooled by the turkey and peppers cut into "noodles"? Add 2 tablespoons plain Greek yogurt when you add the broth and serve over cooked spaghetti or rice noodles for a creamy noodle dish.

BAKED CURRIED CHICKEN AND VEGETABLE RICE

Serves 6 | **Prep time:** 15 minutes / **Cook time:** 55 minutes

DAIRY-FREE, EGG-FREE, GLUTEN-FREE, NUT-FREE, ONE POT

This is the perfect recipe for a busy weeknight family dinner. It's easy, colorful, and bursting with mouthwatering flavors. Cut the ingredients into small pieces for the little ones and they'll love it, too.

4 tablespoons extra-virgin olive oil, divided

1 whole chicken breast, diced

¼ teaspoon sea salt, divided

1 large sweet onion, chopped

1⅓ cups brown rice

8 ounces snap peas, trimmed and cut into pieces

2 carrots, peeled and cut into small pieces

½ head broccoli, cut into florets, chopped, and stems discarded

1 cup chopped cremini mushrooms

4 cups chicken broth

1 tablespoon curry powder

1. Preheat the oven to 400°F.

2. In a Dutch oven or large oven-safe skillet over medium heat, warm 2 tablespoons olive oil. Add the chicken and ⅛ teaspoon salt and brown on each side for 3 minutes. Transfer the chicken to a plate and set aside.

3. Add the remaining 2 tablespoons olive oil and the onion to the Dutch oven and cook for 4 minutes. Add the rice, snap peas, carrots, broccoli, and mushrooms and sauté for 2 minutes. Add the chicken broth, curry, and the remaining ⅛ teaspoon salt, stir well, and bring to a simmer.

4. Cover with a lid and bake for 30 minutes.

5. Add the chicken and continue to bake for an additional 15 minutes, or until the rice is cooked. Serve warm, or cooled to room temperature for toddlers.

Swap it! This is an easy "refrigerator clean up" recipe. The variety of colorful veggies that can make a great combination for the curried chicken is practically endless. Open your refrigerator and use what you have available: bell peppers, asparagus, green beans, summer squash, Brussels sprouts, zucchini, you name it.

THE EASIEST ROAST CHICKEN EVER

Serves 6 | **Prep time:** 10 minutes / **Cook time:** 1½ hours
EGG-FREE, GLUTEN-FREE, NUT-FREE

I used to think that roasting a whole chicken was something elaborate or difficult, but it's really one of the easiest recipes ever and almost impossible to mess up. The juicy and tender roasted chicken with herbs and lemon is perfect for little palates. The prep time is only 10 minutes and the oven does all the heavy lifting, giving you time to spend with the kids. If you can, buy an organic, pasture-raised chicken.

1 whole chicken,
  giblets removed
2 rosemary sprigs
2 marjoram sprigs
1 medium lemon, cut in half
6 cloves garlic, peeled
1 teaspoon sea
  salt, divided
1 tablespoon butter,
  melted, or 2 tablespoons
  extra-virgin olive oil
1 large white onion,
  roughly chopped

1. Preheat the oven to 425°F. Have kitchen twine ready.

2. Rinse the chicken under cold water and pat dry with paper towels. Place the chicken, breast up, in a roasting pan large enough that there are a few inches of space all around the chicken.

3. Place the rosemary, marjoram, lemon halves, garlic, and ½ teaspoon of salt into the cavity.

4. Massage the butter into the breast and legs of the chicken. Season the outside with the remaining ½ teaspoon of salt. Place the onion around the chicken. Tie the legs together with kitchen twine.

5. Roast for 1½ hours, or until cooked through. To check for doneness, make an incision between the leg and thigh. If the meat is still pink, continue to roast, checking every 10 minutes until done.

6. Remove from the oven, cover with parchment paper and a kitchen towel, and let rest for 10 minutes before serving.

Prep help: To prepare a complete meal all in one pan, place the chicken in a bigger roasting pan and add a variety of chopped vegetables around the chicken, such as zucchini, potatoes, squash, eggplant, or carrots.

CREAMY COCONUT AND TURMERIC TURKEY

Serves 4 | **Prep time:** 15 minutes / **Cook time:** 20 minutes
DAIRY-FREE, EGG-FREE, GLUTEN-FREE, NUT-FREE, ONE-POT

Coconut and turmeric? Oh, yes! They will add creaminess and a gorgeous yellow color to this recipe, not to mention the anti-inflammatory and antioxidant properties of turmeric. The flavor of this dish is mild enough that it will please the little ones. Make sure to use full-fat coconut milk for the best flavor and richness. Serve it over brown rice for a complete meal.

2 tablespoons coconut oil

1 yellow onion, diced

4 scallions, finely chopped

2 garlic cloves, minced

1½ pounds turkey breast,
   cut into small pieces

1 (14-ounce) can
   unsweetened
   coconut milk

1 tablespoon tomato paste

2 teaspoons ground
   turmeric

1 teaspoon sea salt

1½ tablespoons
   tapioca starch

2 tablespoons water

1. In a large sauté pan or skillet over medium heat, warm the coconut oil for 1 minute. Add the onion, scallions, and garlic and cook for 2 minutes. Add the turkey and brown for 5 minutes, stirring frequently. Add the coconut milk, tomato paste, turmeric, and salt. Reduce the heat to medium-low and simmer for 8 to 10 minutes.

2. In a small bowl, mix together the tapioca starch with the water and add to the skillet. Mix well and cook for an additional 3 minutes, until the sauce thickens.

Swap it! Turkey or chicken are easily switchable in this recipe, but go a little wild and try shrimp.

Pork and Asparagus Tots with
Tomato Salad, page 116

7

BEYOND THE MEATBALL MEATY MAINS

Red meat is mainly appreciated for its iron content. It is also a great source of lean protein, zinc, and vitamin B_{12}. At the same time, red meat can be associated with high levels of cholesterol and saturated fatty acids. Balance and moderation are key. Offer your toddler (and the whole family) a variety of nutritious foods from every food group, including red meat, and you should get all the nutrients you need.

Red meat can be challenging for toddlers. Some meats require a lot of chewing and can be dry, which is off-putting to them. So when I make a dish with meat, I try to be careful about how the meat is cut, how long it's cooked, and what other ingredients are best combined with it. It could be the difference in your child eating the dish—or not. These are my most successful, kid-approved meaty meals. Enjoy!

Pork and Asparagus Tots with Tomato Salad 116

Wintry Beef and Vegetable Stew 117

Stir-Fried Beef and Spinach 118

Beef and Veggie–Stuffed Zucchini 119

Skillet Steak with Tomato and Olives 120

Bacon, Sweet Pea, and Mushroom Macaroni 121

Apple Rosemary Meatballs with Parmesan Cauliflower Mash 122

Beef and Zucchini Pasta Bolognese 124

Cheesy Beef and Spinach Baked Pasta 126

Pancetta and Provolone Pork Rolls 127

Broccoli and Sausage Risotto 129

Ham and Kale Dumplings 130

PORK AND ASPARAGUS TOTS WITH TOMATO SALAD

Serves 6 | **Prep time:** 15 minutes / **Cook time:** 15 minutes
EGG-FREE, NUT-FREE, 30 MINUTES OR LESS, FREEZER-FRIENDLY

The fresh tomato and iceberg lettuce salad is a nice, light complement to the cute pork and asparagus tots. The beauty of this recipe is that you can make the tots whatever size you want. Make them tiny for the kiddos and make them bigger for mom and dad. They also freeze really well, so you can double the tots part of the recipe and freeze whatever you won't need right away in an airtight container for up to 3 months.

1 pound fresh
  asparagus, trimmed
1 pound ground pork
2 sweet Italian sausages
¼ cup grated
  Parmesan cheese
3 fresh mint leaves, minced
¼ teaspoon sea
  salt, divided
½ cup unbleached all
  purpose flour
6 tablespoons extra-virgin
  olive oil, divided
½ medium head iceberg
  lettuce, shredded
3 heirloom
  tomatoes, chopped
4 fresh basil leaves, minced

1. In a food processor, pulse the asparagus for 30 seconds until it has the consistency of bread-crumbs. Transfer to a large bowl, add the ground pork, sausage, Parmesan cheese, mint, and ⅛ teaspoon salt and mix well to combine.

2. Pour the flour into a shallow bowl. With your hands, form the tots using 1 teaspoon of the pork mixture for each one, and dredge them in the flour.

3. In a large sauté pan or skillet over medium-high heat, warm 3 tablespoons olive oil. Add the tots and cook until browned on all sides, about 5 minutes. Reduce the heat to medium-low and continue cooking for an additional 5 minutes. If the liquid evaporates, you can add 3 tablespoons water to keep the tots from sticking.

4. In a bowl, mix together the lettuce, tomatoes, basil, the remaining 3 tablespoons olive oil, and the remaining ⅛ teaspoon salt.

5. Serve the tots with the salad on the side.

Prep help: If you have weeknights when you have a really tight schedule and only 15 minutes to cook dinner, I suggest preparing the tots the night before and storing them in the refrigerator, ready to be cooked.

WINTRY BEEF AND VEGETABLE STEW

Serves 4 | **Prep time:** 15 minutes / **Cook time:** 45 minutes

DAIRY-FREE, EGG-FREE, NUT-FREE, ONE-POT

There is nothing better than stew when the weather cools down. Traditional stews require hours of simmering, but if you cut the meat into small pieces, the cooking time can be reduced, and you will be able to serve this in less than one hour. To complete the meal, serve with a side of brown rice or try couscous for a Mediterranean twist.

1 pound lean stew
  beef, diced

¼ cup unbleached all
  purpose flour

5 tablespoons extra-virgin
  olive oil, divided

½ white onion, minced

4 potatoes, peeled
  and diced

1½ cups beef broth

Pinch sea salt

7 ounces frozen sweet peas

1 carrot, peeled and diced

1 tablespoon tomato paste

1. In a large bowl, toss the beef with the flour until evenly coated.

2. In a large sauté pan or skillet over medium heat, warm 3 tablespoons olive oil. Add the onion and cook for 2 minutes. Add the beef and sear, stirring frequently, for 3 minutes. Add the potatoes, beef broth, and salt, stir to combine, and cook for 3 minutes. Stir in the peas and diced carrots. Cover and simmer for 35 minutes.

3. Add the tomato paste and the remaining 2 tablespoons olive oil and mix well. Serve warm.

4. **To make it more toddler-friendly:** The ingredients are diced, so most toddlers will find this dish easy to eat, but you can also pulse the cooked stew a few times with an immersion blender, which will make the stew creamier. Serve at room temperature.

Swap it! To make this gluten-free, coat the beef with rice flour or tapioca starch instead of flour.

STIR-FRIED BEEF AND SPINACH

Serves 4 | **Prep time:** 20 minutes / **Cook time:** 10 minutes
DAIRY-FREE, EGG-FREE, NUT-FREE, ONE-POT, 30 MINUTES OR LESS

This makes a lovely weeknight dinner, served on a bed of brown rice or quinoa to complete the meal. The ingredients are probably already in your pantry, but you can make it even more filling by adding mushrooms, snow peas, broccoli, carrots, or even shrimp (make it surf-and-turf night!).

1 pound flank steak or
   sirloin, cut into thin slices
½ cup beef broth
⅓ cup soy sauce
3 tablespoons lemon juice
2 tablespoons
   tapioca starch
1 teaspoon grated
   fresh ginger
1 tablespoon honey
2 tablespoons extra-virgin
   olive oil
2 garlic cloves, minced
3 cups packed
   spinach, chopped

1. In a large bowl, mix together the steak, broth, soy sauce, lemon juice, tapioca starch, ginger, and honey, then cover and place in the refrigerator to marinate for 15 minutes.

2. In a large sauté pan or skillet over medium-high heat, warm the olive oil. Add the garlic and the marinated steak. Reserve the marinade and set aside. Cook, stirring occasionally, until browned, about 3 minutes. Transfer the steak to a bowl and set aside.

3. Add the spinach and the marinade to the skillet and cook, stirring, for 3 minutes. Add the steak back to the skillet, stir, and cook for 1 minute. Serve immediately.

Make it fun. To entice reluctant eaters, let your kids eat their meal using one of those colorful plastic toothpicks used in bento boxes. You can turn it into a game and challenge them to see if they can pick up more than one piece at a time with the toothpick.

BEEF AND VEGGIE–STUFFED ZUCCHINI

Serves 4 | **Prep time:** 15 minutes / **Cook time:** 35 minutes

EGG-FREE, NUT-FREE, FREEZER-FRIENDLY

It's always fun if the bowl your food comes in is also edible! This delicious stuffing is spooned into hollowed-out zucchini shells, which kids really love. After they eat the filling, they can eat the container, too. Once baked, the zucchini can be easily frozen for future meals in an airtight container for up to 3 months.

4 zucchinis

Pinch sea salt

1 red onion, chopped

1 garlic clove

½ pound ground beef

3 tablespoons extra-virgin olive oil, divided

1 eggplant, peeled, hollowed out, and diced

1 carrot, peeled and diced

3 tablespoons grated Parmesan cheese, plus more for topping

4 fresh basil leaves, chopped

1 tablespoon minced fresh parsley

1 to 2 tablespoons breadcrumbs (optional)

1. Preheat the oven to 400°F.

2. Cut the zucchinis in half lengthwise. Then with a spoon, scoop out the insides and place in a food processor. Season the insides of the hollowed-out zucchinis with the salt, place in a baking pan, and set aside.

3. Add the onion and garlic to the food processor and pulse for 10 seconds.

4. Transfer the mixture to a large sauté pan or skillet. Add the ground beef and 2 tablespoons olive oil, and cook, stirring frequently, for 5 minutes. Add the eggplant and carrot to the skillet and continue to cook for 6 more minutes.

5. Remove from the heat. Add the Parmesan cheese, basil, and parsley and stir to combine.

6. If the final mixture is too watery (each zucchini has a different amount of liquid), add 1 or 2 tablespoons of breadcrumbs.

7. Spoon the filling into a hollowed-out zucchini half. Top each zucchini with 1 teaspoon of Parmesan cheese and a drizzle of olive oil and bake for 25 minutes, until cooked through and the cheese starts to brown.

If all else fails . . . Cheese might be the solution. Add 1 cup cheddar cheese to the mixture before filling the zucchini. The final result will be cheesier, gooey, and toddler-approved.

SKILLET STEAK WITH TOMATO AND OLIVES

Serves 4 | **Prep time:** 10 minutes / **Cook time:** 10 minutes
DAIRY-FREE, EGG-FREE, GLUTEN-FREE, NUT-FREE, 30 MINUTES OR LESS

The mix of olives, capers, oregano, and garlic infuse the steak with fresh Mediterranean flavors. For your toddler, make sure to select a very tender skirt steak, and once cooked, slice it into very tiny pieces. Mincing the olives and capers together with the other seasonings will also make this a more toddler-friendly meal.

2 tablespoons chopped
   Taggiasca olives

1 tablespoon capers

1 celery stalk,
   roughly chopped

1 teaspoon dried oregano

3 tablespoons extra-virgin
   olive oil

1 garlic clove

4 skirt steak pieces
   (20 ounces total)

1 cup tomato sauce

Pinch sea salt

1. In a food processor, pulse the olives, capers, celery, and oregano for 10 seconds.

2. In a large sauté pan or skillet over medium heat, warm the olive oil. Add the garlic and cook for 1 minute. Remove the garlic and discard.

3. Increase the heat to medium-high, add the steaks to the skillet, and cook for 3 minutes. Flip the steaks and add the tomato sauce, salt, and olive mixture on top. Reduce the heat to medium-low, cover, and cook for 5 to 6 minutes. Slice and serve immediately.

Swap it! This recipe is delicious made with fish too! Swap out the skirt steak and make it with a sole fillet. The fish has a more delicate texture and can be easier for little ones to eat.

BACON, SWEET PEA, AND MUSHROOM MACARONI

Serves 6 | **Prep time:** 15 minutes / **Cook time:** 10 minutes

EGG-FREE, NUT-FREE, 30 MINUTES OR LESS

Your toddler will love the rich and salty bacon that infuses the mushrooms, making them tastier and easier to please little palates. Mushrooms can be a suspicious ingredient for your toddler, but resist the urge to chop them up. Slice them thinly instead, to keep their shape. It's important that your little ones recognize them, and with time and exposure, they'll realize how delicious mushrooms are.

6 slices bacon (or pancetta or ham), diced

½ yellow onion, minced

3 garlic cloves, minced

1 pound frozen sweet peas

1 cup cremini mushrooms, thinly sliced

1 tablespoon minced fresh parsley

Pinch sea salt

1 pound macaroni pasta

3 tablespoons grated Parmesan cheese, for serving

1. **To make it more toddler-friendly:** Pulse the bacon in a food processor for a few seconds. If the pieces are too big, they might be too chewy for little ones.

2. In a large sauté pan or skillet over medium heat, cook the bacon, onion, and garlic until the bacon is browned, about 5 minutes. Add the peas and mushrooms and stir to combine. Add the parsley and salt, stir, and cook for an additional 5 minutes.

3. Bring a large pot of water to a boil over high heat. Add the pasta and cook according to the package instructions. Drain the pasta, reserving 1 cup of the pasta water.

4. Add the pasta to the mixture in the skillet and stir to combine. If the sauce seems too thick, add the pasta water, 1 tablespoon at a time, until it reaches the desired consistency. Serve with a generous handful of Parmesan cheese on top.

Prep help: To save a little time, you can pulse the bacon, onion, and garlic together in a food processor before adding it to the skillet.

APPLE ROSEMARY MEATBALLS WITH PARMESAN CAULIFLOWER MASH

Serves 6 | **Prep time:** 10 minutes / **Cook time:** 20 minutes
NUT-FREE, 30 MINUTES OR LESS, FREEZER-FRIENDLY

Apples and beef? It may sound like an unusual combination, but the lightly sweet flavor of the apples is perfect for toddlers and appreciated by adults, too. Pink Lady apples have a sweet-tart flavor that goes well with beef, but you can use Fuji or Golden Delicious apples if you can't find them. The cauliflower mash has a creamy, light texture and is a nice alternative to mashed potatoes. I really like it as a side dish with these meatballs. The meatballs are very freezer-friendly. Place them in an airtight container before cooking them and freeze for up to 3 months.

1 pound ground beef

1 Pink Lady apple, peeled, cored, and grated

½ cup breadcrumbs

½ cup milk, divided

1 medium egg

1 garlic clove, minced

1 teaspoon minced fresh parsley

Pinch sea salt

3 tablespoons extra-virgin olive oil

2 small rosemary sprigs

1½ cups water

1 medium head cauliflower cut into florets, chopped, and stems discarded

½ cup grated Parmesan cheese

1. Line a plate with paper towels.

2. In a large bowl, mix together the ground beef, apple, breadcrumbs, ¼ cup milk, egg, garlic, parsley, and salt and thoroughly combine.

3. Using your hands, form 1 tablespoon of the mixture into a ball. Repeat with the rest of the mixture.

4. In a large sauté pan or skillet over medium-high heat, warm the olive oil. Add the meatballs and sear, turning them to cook on all sides, for 3 minutes. Add the rosemary sprigs, reduce the heat to medium-low, and cook for an additional 5 minutes. Transfer the meatballs to the prepared plate. Discard the rosemary.

5. Place a steamer insert in a large pot, add the water, and bring to a boil over high heat. Add the cauliflower to the steamer, reduce the heat to medium, and steam the florets until tender, about 10 minutes.

6. Transfer the cauliflower to a bowl, add the Parmesan cheese and the remaining ¼ cup milk, and mash until the mixture looks like mashed potatoes.

7. Serve the meatballs with spoonfuls of cauliflower mash on the side.

Make it fun. Sometimes I'll spread the cauliflower mash in a circle on my kids' plates and place the meatballs on top to create a smiley face. If you are also serving vegetables as part of the meal, you can arrange veggies like snow peas or green beans to make hair.

BEEF AND ZUCCHINI PASTA BOLOGNESE

Serves 6 | **Prep time:** 10 minutes / **Cook time:** 30 minutes
EGG-FREE, NUT-FREE, FREEZER-FRIENDLY

This is a traditional Bolognese sauce but with a veggie twist. I think it's a great way to combine meat and vegetables, resulting in a lighter, healthier sauce that tastes wonderful. My kids love this sauce, and when I'm cooking, they keep finding reasons to test it, one teaspoon after another. If you prefer an alternative to red meat, use ground turkey or chicken instead. The sauce works really well with tagliatelle pasta, but your toddler might find it difficult to roll the tagliatelle on their fork. Substitute with a short pasta like fusilli, shells, or bowties.

1 yellow onion, minced

1 carrot, peeled
  and minced

1 celery stalk, minced

2 garlic cloves, minced

3 tablespoons extra-virgin
  olive oil

1 pound ground beef

1 pound zucchini, finely
  grated and drained

1 cup tomato sauce

Pinch sea salt, plus
  1 tablespoon, divided

½ cup warm water

1 pound tagliatelle pasta

¼ cup grated Parmesan
  cheese, for serving

1. Pulse the onion, carrot, celery, and garlic in a food processor until minced.

2. In a large sauté pan or skillet over medium heat, warm the olive oil for 1 minute. Add the carrot mixture and cook for 3 minutes. Add the ground beef and cook, stirring frequently, for 5 minutes. Add the zucchini, tomato sauce, salt, and warm water, stir to combine, and bring to a boil. Reduce the heat to medium-low and simmer, uncovered, until the sauce reduces a bit, about 20 minutes.

3. To make it more toddler-friendly: If your toddler likes a super smooth texture, once the Bolognese sauce is cooked, use an immersion blender to transform it into a smooth purée.

4. Fill a large pot with water and bring to a boil over high heat. Add the pasta and the remaining 1 tablespoon salt. Cook according to the package instructions. Drain the pasta, reserving 1 cup of pasta water.

5. Combine the pasta with the Bolognese. If the sauce is too thick, add the reserved pasta water, 1 tablespoon at a time, until it reaches the desired consistency. Serve warm, or cooled to room temperature for toddlers, with a generous handful of Parmesan cheese on top.

Prep help: I usually double this recipe and use what I need for the meal, then freeze the rest in 1- or 2-cup portions that I can use for a variety of future meals.

CHEESY BEEF AND SPINACH BAKED PASTA

Serves 6 | **Prep time:** 20 minutes / **Cook time:** 30 minutes
EGG-FREE, NUT-FREE, FREEZER-FRIENDLY

Spinach meatballs combine with pasta to make a cheesy and comforting baked dish that is appealing for everyone. The combination of flavors alone is toddler-friendly, while the meatballs are loaded with iron and omega-3s to boost the nutritional value of the recipe and make mom happy.

1 pound short pasta, such as elbows or small shells
½ pound ground beef
¼ cup ricotta cheese
3 tablespoons grated Parmesan cheese, plus ½ cup, divided
1 cup frozen spinach, thawed and finely chopped
1 teaspoon garlic powder
¼ teaspoon ground nutmeg
1 tablespoon chia seeds
Pinch sea salt
3 tablespoons extra-virgin olive oil
¾ cup tomato sauce

1. Preheat the oven to 400°F. Have a 9-by-13-inch baking dish ready.

2. Fill a large pot with water and bring to a boil. Cook the pasta for 5 minutes less than the package instructions suggest. Drain, reserving 1 cup of pasta water.

3. In a large bowl, mix together the ground beef, ricotta, 3 tablespoons Parmesan cheese, spinach, garlic, nutmeg, chia seeds, and salt.

4. Using your hands, form 1 tablespoon of the mixture into a ball. Repeat with the rest of the mixture. Place the meatballs in the baking dish. Drizzle the olive oil on top and bake for 20 minutes.

5. Add the pasta and tomato sauce to the baking dish and stir to combine. If the sauce is too thick, add the pasta water, 1 tablespoon at a time, until it reaches the desired consistency. Top with the remaining ½ cup Parmesan cheese.

6. Place the baking dish back in the oven for an additional 10 minutes. Adjust the oven to broil and bake for 3 minutes, until the cheese is golden. Serve hot.

Prep help: Make a double batch of the meatballs and freeze half of them in an airtight container for up to 3 months.

PANCETTA AND PROVOLONE PORK ROLLS

Serves 6 | **Prep time:** 10 minutes / **Cook time:** 20 minutes
EGG-FREE, GLUTEN-FREE, NUT-FREE, ONE-POT, 30 MINUTES OR LESS, FREEZER-FRIENDLY

Sage and rosemary elevate the flavor of these deliciously cheesy pork rolls. For the adults, you can spice up the flavor by adding 2 teaspoons balsamic vinegar in the skillet at the end. For more nutrition, and a more moist pork roll, layer 1 cup thawed and drained frozen spinach with the other fillings.

12 (⅛-inch-thick) pork loin slices

12 slices pancetta

12 slices provolone cheese

12 fresh sage leaves

¼ cup extra-virgin olive oil

2 garlic cloves, cut in half

½ cup chicken broth

2 fresh rosemary sprigs

Pinch sea salt

1. Have 12 to 15 water soaked toothpicks ready.

2. On a clean work surface, lay out the pork slices. Place 1 slice of pancetta, 1 slice of provolone, and 1 sage leaf on top of each slice of pork. Roll up the pork and secure with a toothpick.

3. In a large sauté pan or skillet over medium-high heat, warm the olive oil. Add the garlic and cook for 1 minute. Add the pork rolls and sear, turning to sear all sides, for 4 minutes. Add the broth, rosemary, and salt, then reduce the heat to medium-low and simmer for an additional 15 minutes. Remove the toothpicks and serve.

4. To make it more toddler-friendly: Cut the rolls into thin slices, which will be easier for little ones to chew.

    If all else fails . . . If your toddler likes a softer texture, cook the rolls in 1 cup of tomato sauce. The rolls will be even more tender.

BROCCOLI AND SAUSAGE RISOTTO

Serves 4 | **Prep time:** 15 minutes / **Cook time:** 25 minutes

EGG-FREE, GLUTEN-FREE, NUT-FREE, ONE-POT

Risotto is a great choice for toddlers: The rice releases its starch as it cooks in a savory broth, giving it a creamy, velvety texture. This is my kids' favorite risotto and also mine because the rice, broccoli, and sausage create a balanced and nutritious meal.

5 to 6 cups chicken broth

3 tablespoons extra-virgin olive oil

½ sweet white onion, minced

3 sweet Italian sausages

1 head broccoli, cut into florets, chopped, and stems discarded

1½ cups Arborio or carnaroli rice

¼ cup grated Parmesan cheese

2 tablespoons plain Greek yogurt

1. In a large pot over low heat, warm the broth.

2. In another large pot over medium-high heat, warm the olive oil. Add the onion and cook for 2 minutes. Add the sausage, breaking it up with a spoon, and cook for 2 minutes. Add the broccoli and cook for an additional 2 minutes. Add the rice, stir for 1 minute, and add 3 ladles of broth. Set a timer at 18 minutes.

3. Cook, stirring constantly, until the liquid is almost absorbed. Continue to add the broth, one ladle at a time, letting the liquid absorb after each addition.

4. When the timer goes off, the rice should be cooked. Remove from the heat, add the Parmesan cheese and Greek yogurt, and stir to combine. Serve warm, or cooled to room temperature for toddlers.

Swap it! Risotto is a wonderful base for many ingredient combinations. In addition to sausage and broccoli, I like to use spinach, Swiss chard, zucchini, or asparagus.

HAM AND KALE DUMPLINGS

Serves 4 | **Prep time:** 15 minutes / **Cook time:** 7 minutes
NUT-FREE, 30 MINUTES OR LESS

This is a toddler version of a traditional Italian recipe called *gnudi*, which translates to "naked dumplings." These dumplings are naked because they are not stuffed into pasta. Instead, the eggs bind the kale, cheese, and ham together, and the bread keeps them moist and fluffy.

1 tablespoon sea salt,
   plus extra for sprinkling

1 tablespoon extra-virgin
   olive oil, plus extra for
   drizzling

10 ounces kale, stems
   removed and chopped

7 ounces day-old bread

1 thick slice of ham, diced

2 medium eggs

⅔ cup whole milk

⅔ cup grated Parmesan
   cheese, plus
   2 tablespoons, divided

3 ounces Manchego
   cheese, diced

3 tablespoons
   breadcrumbs

1. Fill a large pot with water. Bring to a boil over high heat and add 1 tablespoon salt. Reduce the heat to keep the water just boiling.

2. In a large sauté pan or skillet over medium-high heat, warm 1 tablespoon olive oil for 1 minute. Add the kale, sprinkle with salt, and cook for 2 to 3 minutes until the volume of the kale reduces to less than half. Let cool for 5 minutes.

3. Transfer the kale to a food processor, add the bread, and process for 1 minute.

4. In a large bowl, mix together the kale mixture, ham, eggs, milk, Parmesan cheese, Manchego cheese, and breadcrumbs.

5. To make it more toddler-friendly: For kids who don't like a lot of texture, add the diced ham to the food processor with the kale and bread, and blend until smooth before mixing with the eggs, milk, cheeses, and breadcrumbs.

6. Using your hands, form small balls and place them on a plate. Add them to the boiling water and cook for 3 minutes. They will rise to the surface of the water when they are cooked. Using a slotted spoon, transfer the dumplings to a serving bowl.

7. Serve with a drizzle of olive oil and a sprinkle of Parmesan cheese.

If all else fails . . . The softness of a boiled dumpling might be challenging for some toddlers. If you know your kiddo won't love the soft texture, pan fry them in a skillet or bake them in a 400°F oven for 15 to 20 minutes. The outside will be crispier and more like a tot. And what toddler doesn't love tots?

Apricot Chia Jam, page 143

8

JUST ADD THIS: DIPS, SAUCES, AND SPREADS

My kids won't eat raw bell peppers. Never. But if bell peppers come with ketchup or mayo, they dig in and crunch every stick. Welcome to the magic world of dips and sauces. The reality is that a tasty dipping sauce increases the chances your toddler will actually eat what you serve them without too much fuss, because the flavors will cover up foods they ordinarily would not eat. But mainly, I think dipping makes eating fun. There are many tasty, ready-to-use dipping sauces at the grocery store, and I do buy them. But I prefer to make them from scratch. They are easy to prepare, they taste fresher, and you don't have to worry about excess sugar, salt, additives, or preservatives.

Avocado Yogurt Dip 134

Asparagus Hummus 135

Healthy Tomato Ketchup 136

Roasted Tomato Sauce 137

Carrot Mayo 139

Zucchini Pesto 140

Creamy Pecan Sauce 141

Almond Cocoa Butter 142

Apricot Chia Jam 143

AVOCADO YOGURT DIP

Makes 1 cup | **Prep time:** 10 minutes

**EGG-FREE, GLUTEN-FREE, NUT-FREE, VEGETARIAN, 30 MINUTES OR LESS,
5 INGREDIENTS OR LESS**

Yogurt is a great ingredient for sauces. It can be combined with pretty much anything and it adds a luscious creaminess to dips. Mixed with avocado, it contains a healthy amount of protein and omega-3s. My kids enjoy this dip with roasted chicken bites or grilled fish fillets.

½ cup plain Greek yogurt

1 Hass avocado, peeled
  and pitted

½ teaspoon minced
  fresh dill

½ teaspoon minced
  fresh chives

Pinch sea salt

1. Place the yogurt, avocado, dill, chives, and salt in a tall container.

2. To make it more toddler-friendly: Reduce the amounts of dill and chives to ¼ teaspoon each, so the flavor will be more delicate.

3. Using an immersion blender, purée the mixture until smooth.

4. Store in an airtight container in the refrigerator for up to 2 days. To prevent the dip from browning, place the avocado pit in the center of the dip. It really works!

Make it fun. Let your toddler help combine the ingredients. They can mash the avocado in a large bowl. Add the rest of the ingredients and let them mix it up. The consistency won't be as smooth as using an immersion blender, but your little one will be so proud!

ASPARAGUS HUMMUS

Makes 2 cups | **Prep time:** 10 minutes / **Cook time:** 20 minutes

DAIRY-FREE, EGG-FREE, NUT-FREE, VEGAN, 30 MINUTES OR LESS

Do your kids love hummus but are a bit bored with the same old recipe? This version with asparagus might tempt them, along with some homemade pita bread chips.

1½ cups water

8 asparagus stalks,
   roughly chopped

1 (15-ounce) can no-salt-
   added chickpeas, drained
   and rinsed

3 tablespoons extra-virgin
   olive oil, divided

1 tablespoon tahini

Zest and juice of 1 lemon

¼ teaspoon sea
   salt, divided

Pita bread, each cut into
   8 wedges

¼ teaspoon dried oregano

1. Preheat the oven to 400°F. Line a baking sheet with parchment paper.

2. In a large pot, bring the water to a boil over high heat. Add the asparagus, reduce the heat to medium, and steam until tender, about 10 minutes.

3. Transfer the asparagus to a food processor, add the chickpeas, 2 tablespoons olive oil, tahini, lemon zest and juice, and ⅛ teaspoon salt and process until smooth.

4. Place the pita wedges on the prepared baking sheet, brush with the remaining 1 tablespoon olive oil, sprinkle with oregano and the remaining ⅛ teaspoon salt, and bake for 10 minutes, until crispy. Let cool.

5. Serve the hummus with pita on the side for dipping. The hummus can be stored in the refrigerator for up to 1 week. The pita can be stored in an airtight container at room temperature for up to 1 week.

Prep help: Instead of using fresh asparagus, you can use frozen. Rinse it under running water to start the thawing process and follow the recipe as instructed.

HEALTHY TOMATO KETCHUP

Makes 2 cups | Prep time: 5 minutes / Cook time: 40 minutes

DAIRY-FREE, EGG-FREE, GLUTEN-FREE, NUT-FREE, VEGAN, ONE-POT

I am addicted to ketchup. So are my hubby and my older child. We will dip anything in ketchup, and because of this, I try to offer it in moderation. Store-bought is fine, but homemade is much better—you can taste the freshness (and I can control the sugar). Maybe we should take it with us when we eat out!

14 ounces tomatoes,
  peeled, seeded,
  and chopped
1/3 cup sweet white
  onion, diced
2 garlic cloves, minced
3 tablespoons maple syrup
2½ tablespoons apple
  cider vinegar
2 tablespoons
  tomato paste
1 teaspoon sea salt
¼ teaspoon mustard
1 teaspoon tapioca starch
1 teaspoon water

1. In a blender, purée the tomatoes, onion, garlic, maple syrup, apple cider vinegar, tomato paste, salt, and mustard for 1 minute, until smooth.

2. Transfer the mixture to a large saucepan over high heat and bring to a boil. Reduce the heat to medium-low and simmer, until the mixture has reduced and thickened, about 30 minutes.

3. In a small cup, mix together the tapioca starch and water to create a paste. Add to the tomato mixture and continue to cook on low heat for an additional 10 minutes. Let cool completely. The ketchup will thicken more as it cools.

4. Transfer to an airtight container and store in the refrigerator for up to 1 month.

Swap it! Fresh tomatoes not in season? You can use 1 (14.5-ounce) can unsalted diced tomatoes and follow the recipe as instructed.

ROASTED TOMATO SAUCE

Makes 6 cups | **Prep time:** 15 minutes / **Cook time:** 60 minutes

DAIRY-FREE, EGG-FREE, GLUTEN-FREE, NUT-FREE, VEGAN, 5 INGREDIENTS OR LESS, FREEZER-FRIENDLY

This is one of our summer favorites. Sun-ripened tomatoes are naturally sweet, and when they are slow-roasted in the oven, the sugars caramelize. Purée them and the result is an incredibly tasty ready-to-use sauce. Your toddler will like it so much that they will want to eat it by the spoonful. It's great as a pasta sauce, or you can spread it on crostini. The sauce can be frozen for up to 6 months, so you can enjoy the taste of summer even in the middle of winter.

2 pounds heirloom tomatoes, seeded and chopped

1 yellow onion, chopped

4 garlic cloves, peeled

5 tablespoons extra-virgin olive oil

1 tablespoon fresh thyme

1 teaspoon sea salt

1. Preheat the oven to 400°F. Have a baking dish ready.

2. In a large bowl, mix together the tomatoes, onion, garlic, olive oil, thyme, and salt. Transfer to the baking dish and bake for 1 hour, stirring once. Let cool.

3. Transfer the mixture to a food processor and process until smooth.

4. Store in an airtight container and freeze for up to 6 months.

Prep help: The quality of the tomatoes is very important. They need to be ripe and sweet. Bite into one to be sure. If you can't find the perfect tomatoes, you can still make the sauce, but if it turns out too acidic, you can add a few tablespoons of milk. For the best results, I would wait until the height of tomato season to make this recipe.

CARROT MAYO

Makes about 1½ cups | **Prep time:** 10 minutes / **Cook time:** 8 minutes

DAIRY-FREE, EGG-FREE, GLUTEN-FREE, NUT-FREE, VEGAN, 30 MINUTES OR LESS,
5 INGREDIENTS OR LESS

This sweet orange mayo is great for toddlers. It's vegan (no worries of egg intolerances) and great with veggies or meat. We love it with steamed broccoli both for the taste and also because kids eat in colors and this dip is beautiful.

4 tablespoons extra-virgin olive oil, divided

3 carrots, peeled and thinly sliced

1 garlic clove, peeled and cut in half

1 bay leaf

Pinch sea salt

½ teaspoon mustard

1 teaspoon apple cider vinegar

1. In a medium sauté pan or skillet over medium-high heat, warm 1 tablespoon olive oil. Reduce the heat to medium. Add the carrots, garlic, bay leaf, and salt and cook for 7 to 8 minutes.

2. Remove and discard the garlic and bay leaf. Transfer the mixture to a food processor. Add the mustard, apple cider vinegar, and the remaining 3 tablespoons olive oil and process until smooth.

3. Store in an airtight container in the refrigerator for up to 3 weeks.

Make it fun. You can drizzle this dip over roasted vegetables or grilled chicken, or pour a few teaspoons in a corner of your toddler's plate so they can try it first before dipping any food. I like serving it in a small cup, saucer, or ramekin, which makes it even more special for kids.

ZUCCHINI PESTO

Makes 1½ cups | Prep time: 15 minutes

EGG-FREE, GLUTEN-FREE, VEGETARIAN, 30 MINUTES OR LESS, 5 INGREDIENTS OR LESS, FREEZER-FRIENDLY

Here is a lighter version of the traditional basil pesto. The zucchini will add body and smooth out the more intense flavors, making it perfect for little palates. It works well as a pasta dressing, but try it as a marinade for chicken or fish.

2 zucchinis, finely grated
  and drained

1 cup packed fresh basil

½ cup grated
  Parmesan cheese

¼ cup pine nuts

5 tablespoons extra-virgin
  olive oil

Pinch sea salt

1. Put the zucchinis, basil, Parmesan cheese, pine nuts, olive oil, and salt in a food processor and blend until smooth.

2. Store in an airtight container in the refrigerator for up to 1 week, or freeze for up to 3 months.

Prep help: To store the pesto in the refrigerator and prevent it from oxidizing, pour a tiny layer of olive oil on top. Your pesto will retain its bright green color.

CREAMY PECAN SAUCE

Makes 3 cups | **Prep time:** 10 minutes
EGG-FREE, VEGETARIAN, 30 MINUTES OR LESS

On crazy weeknights when time is at a premium, pasta recipes are my lifesaver. No matter which kind you choose (durum wheat, rice, quinoa, black beans, red lentil), a yummy sauce will get dinner on the table in no time and—bonus—this one is also nutritious. This Creamy Pecan Sauce has a lovely nutty, cheesy flavor, definitely a toddler favorite, and it's ready in less than 10 minutes.

½ cup crushed pecans

1 small garlic clove, peeled

1 cup grated
   Parmesan cheese

1 cup ricotta cheese

¾ cup milk

6 tablespoons extra-virgin
   olive oil

3 tablespoons
   breadcrumbs

Pinch sea salt

1. Put the pecans and garlic in a food processor and pulse until it has a texture like breadcrumbs.

2. Add the Parmesan, ricotta, milk, olive oil, breadcrumbs, and salt and process until smooth.

3. Store in an airtight container in the refrigerator for up to 1 week, or freeze for up to 3 months.

Swap it! Pecans are my favorite nut to use for this recipe, but you can substitute raw peeled almonds for a sweeter result. For a nut-free alternative, substitute sunflower seeds. The taste will be different but still delicious.

ALMOND COCOA BUTTER

Makes 1½ cups | **Prep time:** 30 minutes
**DAIRY-FREE, EGG-FREE, GLUTEN-FREE, VEGETARIAN, 30 MINUTES OR LESS,
5 INGREDIENTS OR LESS**

This is pure chocolate heaven. Creamy, smooth, and loaded with nutrients, I love offering this homemade spread to my kids in the morning, because it has good fats and proteins that will help them start their day full of energy. Spread it on whole-grain toast or pancakes, serve it with some fresh fruit, or mix it into some oatmeal.

2 cups roasted almonds

2 tablespoons coconut oil

2½ tablespoons
  unsweetened
  cocoa powder

3 tablespoons honey

¼ teaspoon sea salt

1. Put the almonds in a food processor and pulse, stopping to scrape down the sides frequently, for about 20 minutes, or until smooth. Almonds can take a long time to get smooth but start checking at 12 minutes.

2. Add the coconut oil, cocoa powder, honey, and salt and pulse for 2 more minutes, until smooth.

3. Store in an airtight container in the refrigerator for up to 1 month.

If all else fails . . . The great thing about making homemade nut butters is that you can add or remove ingredients depending on your toddler's tastes. To make the butter more appealing for your little one, you can add a few more tablespoons of honey or ½ cup chocolate chips with the almonds at the beginning.

APRICOT CHIA JAM

Makes 2½ cups | **Prep time:** 10 minutes / **Cook time:** 20 minutes

DAIRY-FREE, EGG-FREE, GLUTEN-FREE, NUT-FREE, VEGAN, 30 MINUTES OR LESS, FREEZER-FRIENDLY

Chia fruit jams are a staple in my refrigerator, and I keep them available all year round. Depending on the season, I'll change out the fruit to what's available. Apricots are definitely our favorites, but we also like peaches, plums, apples, pluots, and pears. I prepare a new jam once a month and store it in the refrigerator, so that on busy mornings, all I have to do is spread some almond butter and chia jam on a piece of whole-grain toast for a nutritionally complete breakfast. If you have the time, use cookie cutters to cut the toasts into fun shapes, or give your toddler some sliced fruits to decorate their toast.

1 pound apricots, pitted
  and chopped
1 small Fuji or Pink
  Lady apple, cored
  and chopped
2 tablespoons chia seeds
1 tablespoon lemon zest
⅓ cup water

1. In a medium saucepan over medium-high heat, mix together the apricots, apple, chia seeds, lemon zest, and water and bring to a boil. Reduce the heat to medium-low and simmer, uncovered, stirring occasionally, for 20 minutes.

2. Let cool completely and, using a fork, mash the fruit into a chunky consistency.

3. **To make it more toddler-friendly:** Purée the jam using an immersion blender or food processor for a smoother texture.

4. Store the jam in an airtight container in the refrigerator for up to 2 weeks, or freeze for up to 3 months.

Prep help: The trick of this recipe is to choose almost overripe fruit. They make the jam nice and sweet. Also, be sure you don't peel the apple—the skin contains high levels of pectin, a natural thickener.

Measurement Conversions

	US STANDARD	US STANDARD (OUNCES)	METRIC (APPROXIMATE)
Volume Equivalents (Liquid)	2 tablespoons	1 fl. oz.	30 mL
	¼ cup	2 fl. oz.	60 mL
	½ cup	4 fl. oz.	120 mL
	1 cup	8 fl. oz.	240 mL
	1½ cups	12 fl. oz.	355 mL
	2 cups or 1 pint	16 fl. oz.	475 mL
	4 cups or 1 quart	32 fl. oz.	1 L
	1 gallon	128 fl. oz.	4 L
Volume Equivalents (Dry)	⅛ teaspoon	————	0.5 mL
	¼ teaspoon	————	1 mL
	½ teaspoon	————	2 mL
	¾ teaspoon	————	4 mL
	1 teaspoon	————	5 mL
	1 tablespoon	————	15 mL
	¼ cup	————	59 mL
	⅓ cup	————	79 mL
	½ cup	————	118 mL
	⅔ cup	————	156 mL
	¾ cup	————	177 mL
	1 cup	————	235 mL
	2 cups or 1 pint	————	475 mL
	3 cups	————	700 mL
	4 cups or 1 quart	————	1 L
	½ gallon	————	2 L
	1 gallon	————	4 L
Weight Equivalents	½ ounce	————	15 g
	1 ounce	————	30 g
	2 ounces	————	60 g
	4 ounces	————	115 g
	8 ounces	————	225 g
	12 ounces	————	340 g
	16 ounces or 1 pound	————	455 g

	FAHRENHEIT (F)	CELSIUS (C) (APPROXIMATE)
Oven Temperatures	250°F	120°F
	300°F	150°C
	325°F	180°C
	375°F	190°C
	400°F	200°C
	425°F	220°C
	450°F	230°C

Resources

Websites

Amazon
www.amazon.com

A one-stop shop for everything you'll need for feeding your toddler, from cooking equipment to toddler-friendly utensils and dishes and from specialty ingredients to special-occasion cookie cutters.

Ellyn Satter Institute
https://www.ellynsatterinstitute.org/

Ellyn Satter was a registered dietician and therapist who pioneered the popular "division of responsibility for feeding" method. It's a philosophy that has worked well for my family and eased a lot of stress around mealtimes. The institute's site has plenty of resources and advice for those who want to follow this method.

Healthy Children
https://www.healthychildren.org/English/Pages/default.aspx

This parenting website created by the Academy of American Pediatrics is chock-full of helpful information about all things kids, including feeding and nutrition tips, sample menus, and advice for dealing with a variety of food issues, from picky eating to allergies.

Healthy Kids Association
https://healthy-kids.com.au

This is an Australian organization, but I find their informational resources around raising healthy eaters very helpful and they adapt well for American families.

KidsHealth.org
https://kidshealth.org/en/parents/growth

This nonprofit site has doctor-vetted advice around many kids topics. The Growth and Development section is an invaluable resource on all things feeding and eating.

Zero to Three: Health and Nutrition

https://www.zerotothree.org/early-development/health-and-nutrition

Zero to Three, a national nonprofit dedicated to advancing knowledge and promoting beneficial practices and policies around early childhood, has an excellent website full of resources for parents. The Health and Nutrition section has many helpful articles for any and all topics related to your kids' wellness and nutritional needs.

Books

Aileen Cox Blundell, *The Baby-Led Feeding Cookbook: A New Healthy Way of Eating for Your Baby that the Whole Family Will Love!* Gill Books, 2017.

Aileen is a foodie friend, mom, and my go-to expert for the baby-led weaning method. Her book is loaded with healthy and yummy recipes and tips, if you are following that approach.

Alain Ducasse, *Cooking for Kids: From Babies to Toddlers: Simple, Healthy, and Natural Food.* Rizzoli, 2014.

Alain Ducasse is one of France's best-known chefs. In his book, he approaches baby and toddler food from a healthy haute cuisine perspective.

Alice Callahan, *The Science of Mom: A Research-Based Guide to Your Baby's First Year.* Johns Hopkins University Press, 2015

Alice is a mom and nutritional biologist. Her book is a friendly guide that explains, in easy words loaded with scientific facts, the big questions and topics about babies and toddlers that every parent searches for.

Anthony Porto and Dina DiMaggio, *The Pediatrician's Guide to Feeding Babies and Toddlers: Practical Answers to Your Questions on Nutrition, Starting Solids, Allergies, Picky Eating, and More (For Parents, By Parents).* Ten Speed Press, 2016.

Written by two pediatricians, this guide has all sorts of helpful and practical advice for feeding babies and toddlers.

Ellyn Satter, *Child of Mine: Feeding with Love and Good Sense, Revised and Updated Edition.* Bull Publishing Company, 2000.

Ellyn Satter, *Secrets of Feeding a Healthy Family: How to Eat, How to Raise Good Eaters, How to Cook.* Kelcy Press, 2008.

Ellyn Satter is a recognized authority on children's eating and feeding. Her books are a must-read if you want to approach fussy eating with a positive, proactive, and stress-free attitude.

Kanchan Koya, *Spice Spice Baby: 100 Recipes with Healing Spices for Your Family Table*. Spice Spice Baby LLC, 2018.

Kanchan is a mom and a molecular biologist. She is the queen of spices in the kitchen. Her book will give you tons of recipe ideas for babies and toddlers, while also teaching the healing and health benefits of spices.

Katja Rowell and Jenny McGlothlin, *Helping Your Child with Extreme Picky Eating: A Step-by-Step Guide for Overcoming Selective Eating, Food Aversion, and Feeding Disorders*. New Harbinger Publications, 2015.

Picky eating is a normal phase in childhood, but it can also become a pathology. This is a book you can trust when problems arise and professional help might be needed.

Kelly Dorfman, *Cure Your Child with Food: The Hidden Connection Between Nutrition and Childhood Ailments*. Workman Publishing, 2013.

Kelly is a mom and a pediatric allergy specialist. Through her book, case after case, you will learn the hidden connections between nutritional disorders that affect the body and brain and childhood ailments.

Maryann Jacobsen, *How to Raise a Mindful Eater: 8 Powerful Principles for Transforming Your Child's Relationship with Food*. RMIBooks, 2016.

I would consider this book the shortcut of picky eating books: It's an easy-to-read list of practical suggestions on picky eating.

Nimali Fernando and Melanie Potock, *Raising a Healthy, Happy Eater: A Parent's Handbook: A Stage-by-Stage Guide to Setting Your Child on the Path to Adventurous Eating*. The Experiment, 2015.

This book is written by two excellent feeding therapists and is full of great advice on feeding and picky eating and many real-life stories from their patients through the years.

Tanja Johnston, *The Power of Three: Super Easy PLANT-BASED Recipes for Kids*. Tilda Marleen Verlag, 2014.

Plant-based recipes for your toddler. An interesting approach on the lifelong path to healthy eating.

Index

A

Almond butter
  Orange Quinoa Energy
    Bites, 32
Almond Cocoa Butter, 142
Apples
  Apple Rosemary Meatballs
    with Parmesan Cauliflower
    Mash, 122–123
  Apricot Chia Jam, 143
Apricots
  Apricot Chia Jam, 143
  Orange Quinoa Energy
    Bites, 32
Asparagus
  Asparagus Hummus, 135
  Baked Salmon with
    Asparagus and
    Mushrooms, 86
  Parmesan Roasted
    Asparagus and
    Butternut Squash, 71
  Pork and Asparagus Tots
    with Tomato Salad, 116
  Super Green Frittata
    Bread, 43
Avocados, 12
  Avocado Yogurt Dip, 134
  Cucumber, Tomato, Mango,
    and Avocado Salad, 69
  Green Deviled Eggs, 33
  Healthy Beef and Veggie
    Burgers, 61
  Shrimp and Avocado Salad, 80
  Smoked Salmon, Avocado,
    and Egg Sandwich
    Pockets, 49
  Tomato Avocado
    Sandwiches, 48
  Tuna Panzanella, 81

B

Baby-led weaning, 3
Bacon, Sweet Pea, and
  Mushroom Macaroni, 121
Baked Chicken, Ham, and
  Mozzarella Rolls, 107
Baked Curried Chicken and
  Vegetable Rice, 111
Baked Salmon with Asparagus
  and Mushrooms, 86
Baked Spinach Pasta
  Casserole, 76–77
Bananas
  Chocolaty Zucchini
    Oatmeal, 38
  Immune-Boosting
    Smoothies, 37
  Peanut Butter and Banana
    Smoothies, 35
  Pink Almond Waffles, 40
  Whole-Grain Banana French
    Toast Sticks, 45
Basil
  Beef and Veggie–Stuffed
    Zucchini, 119
  Cucumber, Tomato, Mango,
    and Avocado Salad, 69
  Easy Phyllo Pizzas, 59
  Pork and Asparagus Tots
    with Tomato Salad, 116
  Skillet Mahi-Mahi with Pesto,
    Tomatoes, and Olives, 85
  Super Green Frittata
    Bread, 43
  Tuna Panzanella, 81
  Zucchini Pesto, 140
Beef, 23
  Apple Rosemary Meatballs
    with Parmesan Cauliflower
    Mash, 122–123

Beef and Veggie–Stuffed
  Zucchini, 119
Beef and Zucchini Baked
  Samosas, 56–57
Beef and Zucchini Pasta
  Bolognese, 124–125
Cheesy Beef and Spinach
  Baked Pasta, 126
Healthy Beef and Veggie
  Burgers, 61
Skillet Steak with Tomato
  and Olives, 120
Stir-Fried Beef and
  Spinach, 118
Wintry Beef and
  Vegetable Stew, 117
Beets
  Pink Almond Waffles, 40
Bell peppers
  Focaccia Sandwiches with
    Bell Peppers, Ham, and
    Melted Cheese, 53
  Skillet Turkey and
    Peppers, 109
  Turkey Sausage and
    Zucchini Roll-Ups, 108
Berries
  Blueberry Yogurt Cake, 44
  frozen, 22
  Green Pancakes with
    Blueberries, 41
  Mixed-Berry Chia
    Pudding, 39
  Very Berry Grape
    Smoothies, 34
Blueberry Yogurt Cake, 44
Bowls
  Fish Grain Bowl, 92–93
  Red Lentil and Vegetable
    Bowl, 73

Bowties with Chicken
and Peas, 106
Bread, 12
Super Green Frittata
Bread, 43
Broccoli
Baked Curried Chicken and
Vegetable Rice, 111
Broccoli and Sausage
Risotto, 129
Broccoli Risotto, 75
Chicken and Broccoli
Meatballs in Tomato
Sauce, 104–105
Fish Grain Bowl, 92–93
Quinoa Veggie Croquettes, 64
Roasted Broccoli and
Ricotta Sandwiches, 52
Roasted Chicken and
Vegetable Quinoa
Salad, 98–99
Salmon and Broccoli Fusilli, 83
Bulgur
Sole and Bulgur–Stuffed
Tomatoes, 88–89

C
Cabbage
Purple Cabbage
Potato Salad, 70
Red Lentil and Vegetable
Bowl, 73
Carbohydrates, 4
Carrots, 12
Baked Chicken, Ham, and
Mozzarella Rolls, 107
Baked Curried Chicken and
Vegetable Rice, 111
Beef and Veggie–Stuffed
Zucchini, 119
Beef and Zucchini Pasta
Bolognese, 124–125
Carrot Mayo, 139
Chicken Soup for a
Cold, 100–101

Cream of Carrot and
Lentil Soup, 67
Healthy Beef and Veggie
Burgers, 61
Pesto Chicken Pinwheels, 102
Quinoa Veggie Croquettes, 64
Red Lentil and Vegetable
Bowl, 73
Roasted Broccoli and
Ricotta Sandwiches, 52
Roasted Chicken and
Vegetable Quinoa
Salad, 98–99
Vegetable Minestrone, 65
Wintry Beef and
Vegetable Stew, 117
Cauliflower
Apple Rosemary Meatballs
with Parmesan Cauliflower
Mash, 122–123
Cauliflower and Fish
Croquettes, 82
Vegetable Minestrone, 65
Very Berry Grape
Smoothies, 34
Celery
Beef and Zucchini Pasta
Bolognese, 124–125
Chicken Soup for a
Cold, 100–101
Skillet Steak with Tomato
and Olives, 120
Cheese. See specific, 12
Cheesy Beef and Spinach
Baked Pasta, 126
Chia seeds
Apricot Chia Jam, 143
Cheesy Beef and Spinach
Baked Pasta, 126
Chicken and Broccoli
Meatballs in Tomato
Sauce, 104–105
Chocolaty Zucchini
Oatmeal, 38
Mixed-Berry Chia Pudding, 39

Chicken, 22, 97
Baked Chicken, Ham, and
Mozzarella Rolls, 107
Baked Curried Chicken and
Vegetable Rice, 111
Bowties with Chicken
and Peas, 106
Chicken and Broccoli
Meatballs in Tomato
Sauce, 104–105
Chicken Soup for a
Cold, 100–101
The Easiest Roast
Chicken Ever, 112
Nuggets, 12
Pesto Chicken Pinwheels, 102
Quinoa Chicken Bites, 103
Roasted Chicken and
Vegetable Quinoa
Salad, 98–99
Chickpeas
Asparagus Hummus, 135
Chives
Avocado Yogurt Dip, 134
Chocolate, 13
Almond Cocoa Butter, 142
Chocolaty Zucchini
Oatmeal, 38
Orange Quinoa Energy
Bites, 32
Choking hazards, 8
Cilantro
Fish Grain Bowl, 92–93
Cocoa, unsweetened, 21
Coconut
Orange Quinoa Energy
Bites, 32
Coconut milk/cream
Cream of Carrot and
Lentil Soup, 67
Creamy Coconut and
Turmeric Turkey, 113
Mixed-Berry Chia
Pudding, 39
Coconut oil, 20

Cod and Zucchini Shells
        Pasta, 84
Cooking with kids, 15–16
Corn
    Shrimp and Avocado
        Salad, 80
    Tomato and Cheese
        Tortilla Cups, 54
    Tuna Panzanella, 81
Couscous
    Fish Grain Bowl, 92–93
Cream cheese
    Turkey Sausage and
        Zucchini Roll-Ups, 108
    Zucchini and Ham Roll-Ups, 50
Cream of Carrot and
        Lentil Soup, 67
Creamy Coconut and
        Turmeric Turkey, 113
Creamy Pecan Sauce, 141
Cucumbers
    Cucumber, Tomato, Mango,
        and Avocado Salad, 69
    Roasted Broccoli and
        Ricotta Sandwiches, 52
    Tuna Panzanella, 81

D

Dairy-free
    Almond Cocoa Butter, 142
    Apricot Chia Jam, 143
    Asparagus Hummus, 135
    Baked Curried Chicken and
        Vegetable Rice, 111
    Baked Salmon with Asparagus
        and Mushrooms, 86
    Beef and Zucchini Baked
        Samosas, 56–57
    Carrot Mayo, 139
    Cauliflower and Fish
        Croquettes, 82
    Chocolaty Zucchini
        Oatmeal, 38
    Cod and Zucchini
        Shells Pasta, 84

Cream of Carrot and
        Lentil Soup, 67
Creamy Coconut and
        Turmeric Turkey, 113
Cucumber, Tomato, Mango,
        and Avocado Salad, 69
The Easiest Roast
        Chicken Ever, 112
Green Deviled Eggs, 33
Healthy Tomato Ketchup, 136
Immune-Boosting
        Smoothies, 37
Mixed-Berry Chia Pudding, 39
Orange Quinoa Energy
        Bites, 32
Purple Cabbage
        Potato Salad, 70
Roasted Chicken and
        Vegetable Quinoa
        Salad, 98–99
Roasted Tomato Sauce, 137
Salmon and Zucchini
        Skewers, 91
Shrimp and Avocado Salad, 80
Shrimp-Stuffed Zucchini
        Boats, 87
Skillet Steak with Tomato
        and Olives, 120
Skillet Turkey and
        Peppers, 109
Smoked Salmon, Avocado,
        and Egg Sandwich
        Pockets, 49
Sole and Bulgur–Stuffed
        Tomatoes, 88–89
Stir-Fried Beef and
        Spinach, 118
Tomato Avocado
        Sandwiches, 48
Tuna Panzanella, 81
Turkey, Tomato, and Pesto
        Pita Pockets, 55
Vegetable Minestrone, 65
Whole-Grain Banana French
        Toast Sticks, 45

Wintry Beef and
        Vegetable Stew, 117
Dairy products, 6
Dates
    Orange Quinoa Energy
        Bites, 32
Dill
    Avocado Yogurt Dip, 134
    Salmon and Zucchini
        Skewers, 91
Dips and spreads
    Almond Cocoa Butter, 142
    Apricot Chia Jam, 143
    Asparagus Hummus, 135
    Avocado Yogurt Dip, 134
    Carrot Mayo, 139
    Healthy Tomato Ketchup, 136
    Zucchini Pesto, 140
"Division of Responsibility"
        approach, 18

E

The Easiest Roast Chicken
        Ever, 112
Easy Phyllo Pizzas, 59
Edamame, 22
    Fish Grain Bowl, 92–93
    Super Green Frittata Bread, 43
Egg-free
    Almond Cocoa Butter, 142
    Apricot Chia Jam, 143
    Asparagus Hummus, 135
    Avocado Yogurt Dip, 134
    Bacon, Sweet Pea, and
        Mushroom Macaroni, 121
    Baked Chicken, Ham, and
        Mozzarella Rolls, 107
    Baked Curried Chicken and
        Vegetable Rice, 111
    Baked Salmon with Asparagus
        and Mushrooms, 86
    Baked Spinach Pasta
        Casserole, 76–77
    Beef and Veggie–Stuffed
        Zucchini, 119

Egg-free (Continued)
Beef and Zucchini Baked
Samosas, 56–57
Beef and Zucchini Pasta
Bolognese, 124–125
Bowties with Chicken
and Peas, 106
Broccoli and Sausage
Risotto, 129
Broccoli Risotto, 75
Carrot Mayo, 139
Cheesy Beef and Spinach
Baked Pasta, 126
Chicken and Broccoli
Meatballs in Tomato
Sauce, 104–105
Chicken Soup for a
Cold, 100–101
Chocolaty Zucchini
Oatmeal, 38
Cod and Zucchini
Shells Pasta, 84
Cream of Carrot and
Lentil Soup, 67
Creamy Coconut and
Turmeric Turkey, 113
Creamy Pecan Sauce, 141
Cucumber, Tomato, Mango,
and Avocado Salad, 69
The Easiest Roast
Chicken Ever, 112
Easy Phyllo Pizzas, 59
Eggplant, Tomato, and
Feta Pasta, 74
Fennel Leek Soup with
Parmesan Chips, 66
Focaccia Sandwiches with
Bell Peppers, Ham, and
Melted Cheese, 53
Ham and Cheese
Calzones, 51
Healthy Tomato Ketchup, 136
Immune-Boosting
Smoothies, 37
Mixed-Berry Chia Pudding, 39

Orange Quinoa Energy
Bites, 32
Pancetta and Provolone
Pork Rolls, 127
Parmesan Roasted Asparagus
and Butternut Squash, 71
Peanut Butter and Banana
Smoothies, 35
Pesto Chicken Pinwheels, 102
Polenta Pizza Squares, 58
Pork and Asparagus Tots
with Tomato Salad, 116
Purple Cabbage
Potato Salad, 70
Red Lentil and Vegetable
Bowl, 73
Roasted Broccoli and
Ricotta Sandwiches, 52
Roasted Chicken and
Vegetable Quinoa
Salad, 98–99
Roasted Tomato Sauce, 137
Salmon and Broccoli Fusilli, 83
Salmon and Zucchini
Skewers, 91
Sheet Pan Tilapia with
Potatoes, Tomatoes,
and Olives, 94–95
Shrimp and Avocado Salad, 80
Shrimp-Stuffed Zucchini
Boats, 87
Skillet Mahi-Mahi with Pesto,
Tomatoes, and Olives, 85
Skillet Steak with Tomato
and Olives, 120
Skillet Turkey and
Peppers, 109
Sole and Bulgur–Stuffed
Tomatoes, 88–89
Spaghetti and Zoodles, 72
Stir-Fried Beef and
Spinach, 118
Tomato and Cheese
Tortilla Cups, 54
Tuna Panzanella, 81

Turkey, Tomato, and Pesto
Pita Pockets, 55
Turkey Sausage and
Zucchini Roll-Ups, 108
Vegetable Minestrone, 65
Very Berry Grape
Smoothies, 34
Wintry Beef and
Vegetable Stew, 117
Zucchini and Ham Roll-Ups, 50
Zucchini Pesto, 140
Eggplants
Beef and Veggie–Stuffed
Zucchini, 119
Eggplant, Tomato, and
Feta Pasta, 74
Eggs, 22
Green Deviled Eggs, 33
Smoked Salmon, Avocado,
and Egg Sandwich
Pockets, 49
Whole-Grain Banana French
Toast Sticks, 45
Equipment, 25–26

F
Family meals, 2
Fats, 4, 6
Fennel Leek Soup with
Parmesan Chips, 66
Feta cheese
Eggplant, Tomato, and
Feta Pasta, 74
Fiber, 4
Fish, 23
Baked Salmon with Asparagus
and Mushrooms, 86
Cauliflower and Fish
Croquettes, 82
Cod and Zucchini
Shells Pasta, 84
Fish Grain Bowl, 92–93
Salmon and Broccoli Fusilli, 83
Salmon and Zucchini
Skewers, 91

Sheet Pan Tilapia with Potatoes, Tomatoes, and Olives, 94–95
Skillet Mahi-Mahi with Pesto, Tomatoes, and Olives, 85
Smoked Salmon, Avocado, and Egg Sandwich Pockets, 49
Sole and Bulgur–Stuffed Tomatoes, 88–89
Tuna Panzanella, 81
5 ingredients or less
  Almond Cocoa Butter, 142
  Avocado Yogurt Dip, 134
  Carrot Mayo, 139
  Cucumber, Tomato, Mango, and Avocado Salad, 69
  Focaccia Sandwiches with Bell Peppers, Ham, and Melted Cheese, 53
  Green Deviled Eggs, 33
  Ham and Cheese Calzones, 51
  Mixed-Berry Chia Pudding, 39
  Parmesan Roasted Asparagus and Butternut Squash, 71
  Purple Cabbage Potato Salad, 70
  Roasted Broccoli and Ricotta Sandwiches, 52
  Roasted Tomato Sauce, 137
  Skillet Mahi-Mahi with Pesto, Tomatoes, and Olives, 85
  Smoked Salmon, Avocado, and Egg Sandwich Pockets, 49
  Sole and Bulgur–Stuffed Tomatoes, 88–89
  Tomato Avocado Sandwiches, 48
  Turkey, Tomato, and Pesto Pita Pockets, 55
  Whole-Grain Banana French Toast Sticks, 45
  Zucchini and Ham Roll-Ups, 50
  Zucchini Pesto, 140

Flours, 20
Focaccia Sandwiches with Bell Peppers, Ham, and Melted Cheese, 53
Food allergies, 9
Food labels, 24
Food-themed activities, 19
Freezer-friendly
  Apple Rosemary Meatballs with Parmesan Cauliflower Mash, 122–123
  Apricot Chia Jam, 143
  Beef and Veggie–Stuffed Zucchini, 119
  Beef and Zucchini Baked Samosas, 56–57
  Beef and Zucchini Pasta Bolognese, 124–125
  Cheesy Beef and Spinach Baked Pasta, 126
  Chicken and Broccoli Meatballs in Tomato Sauce, 104–105
  Chicken Soup for a Cold, 100–101
  Easy Phyllo Pizzas, 59
  Healthy Beef and Veggie Burgers, 61
  Pancetta and Provolone Pork Rolls, 127
  Pork and Asparagus Tots with Tomato Salad, 116
  Roasted Tomato Sauce, 137
  Super Green Frittata Bread, 43
  Zucchini Pesto, 140
Freezer staples, 22–23
Fruits, 6, 20. *See also specific*

G

Gluten-free
  Almond Cocoa Butter, 142
  Apricot Chia Jam, 143
  Avocado Yogurt Dip, 134
  Baked Chicken, Ham, and Mozzarella Rolls, 107

Baked Curried Chicken and Vegetable Rice, 111
Baked Salmon with Asparagus and Mushrooms, 86
Beef and Veggie–Stuffed Zucchini, 119
Broccoli and Sausage Risotto, 129
Broccoli Risotto, 75
Carrot Mayo, 139
Chocolaty Zucchini Oatmeal, 38
Cream of Carrot and Lentil Soup, 67
Creamy Coconut and Turmeric Turkey, 113
Cucumber, Tomato, Mango, and Avocado Salad, 69
The Easiest Roast Chicken Ever, 112
Fennel Leek Soup with Parmesan Chips, 66
Green Deviled Eggs, 33
Healthy Tomato Ketchup, 136
Immune-Boosting Smoothies, 37
Mixed-Berry Chia Pudding, 39
Orange Quinoa Energy Bites, 32
Pancetta and Provolone Pork Rolls, 127
Parmesan Roasted Asparagus and Butternut Squash, 71
Peanut Butter and Banana Smoothies, 35
Pesto Chicken Pinwheels, 102
Pink Almond Waffles, 40
Polenta Pizza Squares, 58
Purple Cabbage Potato Salad, 70
Quinoa Chicken Bites, 103
Red Lentil and Vegetable Bowl, 73

Gluten-free *(Continued)*
    Roasted Chicken and
        Vegetable Quinoa
        Salad, 98–99
    Roasted Tomato Sauce, 137
    Salmon and Zucchini
        Skewers, 91
    Shrimp and Avocado
        Salad, 80
    Skillet Mahi-Mahi with Pesto,
        Tomatoes, and Olives, 85
    Skillet Steak with Tomato
        and Olives, 120
    Skillet Turkey and
        Peppers, 109
    Turkey Sausage and
        Zucchini Roll-Ups, 108
    Vegetable Minestrone, 65
    Very Berry Grape
        Smoothies, 34
    Zucchini and Ham Roll-Ups, 50
    Zucchini Pesto, 140
Gouda cheese
    Pesto Chicken Pinwheels, 102
Grains, 6, 21
Grapes
    Very Berry Grape
        Smoothies, 34
Greek yogurt, 22
    Avocado Yogurt Dip, 134
    Blueberry Yogurt Cake, 44
    Broccoli and Sausage
        Risotto, 129
    Broccoli Risotto, 75
    Fish Grain Bowl, 92–93
    Peanut Butter and Banana
        Smoothies, 35
Green Deviled Eggs, 33
Green Pancakes with
    Blueberries, 41

H

Ham
    Baked Chicken, Ham, and
        Mozzarella Rolls, 107

Focaccia Sandwiches with
    Bell Peppers, Ham, and
    Melted Cheese, 53
Ham and Cheese
    Calzones, 51
Ham and Kale
    Dumplings, 130–131
Savory Breakfast Cookies, 42
Zucchini and Ham Roll-Ups, 50
Healthy Beef and Veggie
    Burgers, 61
Healthy Tomato Ketchup, 136
Herbs, 20. *See also*
    specific fresh
Honey, 8

I

Immune-Boosting
    Smoothies, 37
Iron, 4

K

Kale
    Cream of Carrot and
        Lentil Soup, 67
    Ham and Kale
        Dumplings, 130–131
    Immune-Boosting
        Smoothies, 37
    Red Lentil and Vegetable
        Bowl, 73
Kefir, 22
    Very Berry Grape
        Smoothies, 34

L

Leeks
    Bowties with Chicken
        and Peas, 106
    Fennel Leek Soup with
        Parmesan Chips, 66
    Vegetable Minestrone, 65
Lentils
    Cream of Carrot and
        Lentil Soup, 67

    Red Lentil and Vegetable
        Bowl, 73
Lettuce
    Healthy Beef and Veggie
        Burgers, 61
    Pork and Asparagus Tots
        with Tomato Salad, 116

M

Macronutrients, 4
Manchego cheese
    Ham and Kale
        Dumplings, 130–131
    Tomato and Cheese
        Tortilla Cups, 54
Mangos
    Cucumber, Tomato, Mango,
        and Avocado Salad, 69
    Immune-Boosting
        Smoothies, 37
Meal planning, 14–15
Mealtimes, 16–17. *See also*
    Family meals
Meat, 115
Milk, 22
Mint
    Beef and Zucchini Baked
        Samosas, 56–57
    Cucumber, Tomato, Mango,
        and Avocado Salad, 69
    Pork and Asparagus Tots
        with Tomato Salad, 116
    Shrimp-Stuffed Zucchini
        Boats, 87
Mixed-Berry Chia
    Pudding, 39
Modeling healthy eating, 10
Mozzarella cheese
    Baked Chicken, Ham, and
        Mozzarella Rolls, 107
    Easy Phyllo Pizzas, 59
    Polenta Pizza Squares, 58
Mushrooms
    Bacon, Sweet Pea, and
        Mushroom Macaroni, 121

Baked Curried Chicken and
Vegetable Rice, 111
Baked Salmon with Asparagus
and Mushrooms, 86
Healthy Beef and Veggie
Burgers, 61

N

Nut butters, 20
Nut-free
Apple Rosemary Meatballs
with Parmesan Cauliflower
Mash, 122–123
Apricot Chia Jam, 143
Asparagus Hummus, 135
Avocado Yogurt Dip, 134
Bacon, Sweet Pea, and
Mushroom Macaroni, 121
Baked Curried Chicken and
Vegetable Rice, 111
Baked Salmon with
Asparagus and
Mushrooms, 86
Beef and Veggie–Stuffed
Zucchini, 119
Beef and Zucchini Baked
Samosas, 56–57
Beef and Zucchini Pasta
Bolognese, 124–125
Blueberry Yogurt Cake, 44
Bowties with Chicken
and Peas, 106
Broccoli and Sausage
Risotto, 129
Broccoli Risotto, 75
Carrot Mayo, 139
Cheesy Beef and Spinach
Baked Pasta, 126
Chicken and Broccoli
Meatballs in Tomato
Sauce, 104–105
Chicken Soup for a
Cold, 100–101
Chocolaty Zucchini
Oatmeal, 38

Cream of Carrot and
Lentil Soup, 67
Creamy Coconut and
Turmeric Turkey, 113
Cucumber, Tomato, Mango,
and Avocado Salad, 69
The Easiest Roast
Chicken Ever, 112
Easy Phyllo Pizzas, 59
Fennel Leek Soup with
Parmesan Chips, 66
Focaccia Sandwiches with
Bell Peppers, Ham, and
Melted Cheese, 53
Green Deviled Eggs, 33
Green Pancakes with
Blueberries, 41
Ham and Cheese Calzones, 51
Ham and Kale
Dumplings, 130–131
Healthy Beef and Veggie
Burgers, 61
Healthy Tomato Ketchup, 136
Immune-Boosting
Smoothies, 37
Mixed-Berry Chia Pudding, 39
Pancetta and Provolone
Pork Rolls, 127
Parmesan Roasted Asparagus
and Butternut Squash, 71
Polenta Pizza Squares, 58
Pork and Asparagus Tots
with Tomato Salad, 116
Purple Cabbage
Potato Salad, 70
Quinoa Chicken Bites, 103
Quinoa Veggie Croquettes, 64
Red Lentil and Vegetable
Bowl, 73
Roasted Broccoli and
Ricotta Sandwiches, 52
Roasted Chicken and
Vegetable Quinoa
Salad, 98–99
Roasted Tomato Sauce, 137

Salmon and Broccoli Fusilli, 83
Salmon and Zucchini
Skewers, 91
Savory Breakfast Cookies, 42
Shrimp and Avocado
Salad, 80
Shrimp-Stuffed Zucchini
Boats, 87
Skillet Steak with Tomato
and Olives, 120
Skillet Turkey and
Peppers, 109
Smoked Salmon, Avocado,
and Egg Sandwich
Pockets, 49
Sole and Bulgur–Stuffed
Tomatoes, 88–89
Spaghetti and Zoodles, 72
Stir-Fried Beef and
Spinach, 118
Super Green Frittata Bread, 43
Tomato and Cheese
Tortilla Cups, 54
Tomato Avocado
Sandwiches, 48
Tuna Panzanella, 81
Turkey Sausage and
Zucchini Roll-Ups, 108
Vegetable Minestrone, 65
Very Berry Grape
Smoothies, 34
Whole-Grain Banana French
Toast Sticks, 45
Wintry Beef and
Vegetable Stew, 117
Zucchini and Ham Roll-Ups, 50
Nuts, 20. *See also specific*

O

Oats
Chocolaty Zucchini
Oatmeal, 38
Peanut Butter and Banana
Smoothies, 35
Olive oil, 21

Olives
  Easy Phyllo Pizzas, 59
  Eggplant, Tomato, and
    Feta Pasta, 74
  Polenta Pizza Squares, 58
  Sheet Pan Tilapia with
    Potatoes, Tomatoes,
    and Olives, 94–95
  Skillet Mahi-Mahi with Pesto,
    Tomatoes, and Olives, 85
  Skillet Steak with Tomato
    and Olives, 120
  Tuna Panzanella, 81
Omega-3 fatty acids, 4
One-pot
  Baked Chicken, Ham, and
    Mozzarella Rolls, 107
  Baked Curried Chicken and
    Vegetable Rice, 111
  Baked Salmon with
    Asparagus and
    Mushrooms, 86
  Broccoli and Sausage
    Risotto, 129
  Broccoli Risotto, 75
  Chicken Soup for a
    Cold, 100–101
  Cream of Carrot and
    Lentil Soup, 67
  Creamy Coconut and
    Turmeric Turkey, 113
  Fennel Leek Soup with
    Parmesan Chips, 66
  Healthy Tomato Ketchup, 136
  Pancetta and Provolone
    Pork Rolls, 127
  Parmesan Roasted
    Asparagus and
    Butternut Squash, 71
  Pesto Chicken Pinwheels, 102
  Red Lentil and Vegetable
    Bowl, 73
  Roasted Chicken and
    Vegetable Quinoa
    Salad, 98–99

Sheet Pan Tilapia with
  Potatoes, Tomatoes,
  and Olives, 94–95
Skillet Mahi-Mahi with
  Pesto, Tomatoes,
  and Olives, 85
Skillet Turkey and
  Peppers, 109
Stir-Fried Beef and
  Spinach, 118
Vegetable Minestrone, 65
Wintry Beef and
  Vegetable Stew, 117
Oranges
  Blueberry Yogurt Cake, 44
  Orange Quinoa Energy
    Bites, 32
Organic foods, 24

P
Pancetta and Provolone
  Pork Rolls, 127
Pantry staples, 20–21
Parmesan cheese, 22
  Apple Rosemary Meatballs
    with Parmesan Cauliflower
    Mash, 122–123
  Bacon, Sweet Pea, and
    Mushroom Macaroni, 121
  Baked Spinach Pasta
    Casserole, 76–77
  Beef and Veggie–Stuffed
    Zucchini, 119
  Beef and Zucchini Pasta
    Bolognese, 124–125
  Bowties with Chicken
    and Peas, 106
  Broccoli and Sausage
    Risotto, 129
  Broccoli Risotto, 75
  Cheesy Beef and Spinach
    Baked Pasta, 126
  Chicken and Broccoli
    Meatballs in Tomato
    Sauce, 104–105

Chicken Soup for a
  Cold, 100–101
Creamy Pecan Sauce, 141
Fennel Leek Soup with
  Parmesan Chips, 66
Ham and Kale
  Dumplings, 130–131
Healthy Beef and Veggie
  Burgers, 61
Parmesan Roasted Asparagus
  and Butternut Squash, 71
Pork and Asparagus Tots
  with Tomato Salad, 116
Quinoa Chicken Bites, 103
Quinoa Veggie Croquettes, 64
Savory Breakfast Cookies, 42
Sheet Pan Tilapia with
  Potatoes, Tomatoes,
  and Olives, 94–95
Spaghetti and Zoodles, 72
Super Green Frittata Bread, 43
Vegetable Minestrone, 65
Zucchini Pesto, 140
Parmesan Roasted Asparagus
  and Butternut Squash, 71
Parsnips
  Chicken Soup for a
    Cold, 100–101
Pasta, 13, 21
  Bacon, Sweet Pea, and
    Mushroom Macaroni, 121
  Baked Spinach Pasta
    Casserole, 76–77
  Beef and Zucchini Pasta
    Bolognese, 124–125
  Bowties with Chicken
    and Peas, 106
  Cheesy Beef and Spinach
    Baked Pasta, 126
  Chicken Soup for a
    Cold, 100–101
  Cod and Zucchini
    Shells Pasta, 84
  Eggplant, Tomato, and
    Feta Pasta, 74

Salmon and Broccoli Fusilli, 83
Spaghetti and Zoodles, 72
Peanut Butter and Banana
    Smoothies, 35
Pears
    Immune-Boosting
        Smoothies, 37
Peas, 23
    Bacon, Sweet Pea, and
        Mushroom Macaroni, 121
    Baked Curried Chicken and
        Vegetable Rice, 111
    Bowties with Chicken
        and Peas, 106
    Sheet Pan Tilapia with
        Potatoes, Tomatoes,
        and Olives, 94–95
    Super Green Frittata
        Bread, 43
    Wintry Beef and
        Vegetable Stew, 117
Pecan Sauce, Creamy, 141
Pesto
    Pesto Chicken Pinwheels, 102
    Skillet Mahi-Mahi with Pesto,
        Tomatoes, and Olives, 85
    Turkey, Tomato, and Pesto
        Pita Pockets, 55
    Zucchini Pesto, 140
Picky eating, 7
Pineapple
    Immune-Boosting
        Smoothies, 37
Pine nuts
    Eggplant, Tomato, and
        Feta Pasta, 74
    Zucchini Pesto, 140
Pink Almond Waffles, 40
Pizza, 13
    Easy Phyllo Pizzas, 59
    Polenta Pizza Squares, 58
Polenta Pizza Squares, 58
Pork. See also Ham
    Bacon, Sweet Pea, and
        Mushroom Macaroni, 121

Broccoli and Sausage
    Risotto, 129
Pancetta and Provolone
    Pork Rolls, 127
Pork and Asparagus Tots
    with Tomato Salad, 116
Portion size, 5
Potatoes
    Purple Cabbage
        Potato Salad, 70
    Red Lentil and Vegetable
        Bowl, 73
    Sheet Pan Tilapia with
        Potatoes, Tomatoes,
        and Olives, 94–95
    Vegetable Minestrone, 65
    Wintry Beef and
        Vegetable Stew, 117
Proteins, 4, 6
Provolone cheese
    Focaccia Sandwiches with
        Bell Peppers, Ham, and
        Melted Cheese, 53
    Ham and Cheese Calzones, 51
    Pancetta and Provolone
        Pork Rolls, 127
    Purple Cabbage Potato
        Salad, 70

Q

Quinoa
    Orange Quinoa Energy
        Bites, 32
    Quinoa Chicken Bites, 103
    Quinoa Veggie Croquettes, 64
    Roasted Chicken and
        Vegetable Quinoa
        Salad, 98–99

R

Recipes, about, 27–28
Red Lentil and Vegetable
    Bowl, 73
Refrigerator staples, 22
Rice, 21

Baked Curried Chicken and
    Vegetable Rice, 111
Broccoli and Sausage
    Risotto, 129
Broccoli Risotto, 75
Ricotta cheese
    Baked Spinach Pasta
        Casserole, 76–77
    Cheesy Beef and Spinach
        Baked Pasta, 126
    Creamy Pecan Sauce, 141
    Roasted Broccoli and
        Ricotta Sandwiches, 52
Roasted Broccoli and Ricotta
    Sandwiches, 52
Roasted Chicken and Vegetable
    Quinoa Salad, 98–99
Roasted Tomato Sauce, 137
Rosemary
    Apple Rosemary Meatballs
        with Parmesan Cauliflower
        Mash, 122–123
    The Easiest Roast
        Chicken Ever, 112
    Pancetta and Provolone
        Pork Rolls, 127
    Roasted Chicken and
        Vegetable Quinoa
        Salad, 98–99
    Vegetable Minestrone, 65

S

Safety, 16
Sage
    Baked Chicken, Ham, and
        Mozzarella Rolls, 107
    Pancetta and Provolone
        Pork Rolls, 127
    Tomato and Cheese
        Tortilla Cups, 54
    Turkey Sausage and
        Zucchini Roll-Ups, 108
Salads
    Cucumber, Tomato, Mango,
        and Avocado Salad, 69

Salads *(Continued)*
  Purple Cabbage
    Potato Salad, 70
  Roasted Chicken and
    Vegetable Quinoa
    Salad, 98–99
  Shrimp and Avocado Salad, 80
  Tuna Panzanella, 81
Salmon, 23
  Baked Salmon with Asparagus
    and Mushrooms, 86
  Salmon and Broccoli Fusilli, 83
  Salmon and Zucchini
    Skewers, 91
  Smoked Salmon, Avocado,
    and Egg Sandwich
    Pockets, 49
Salt, 9
Sandwiches and wraps
  Beef and Zucchini Baked
    Samosas, 56–57
  Focaccia Sandwiches with
    Bell Peppers, Ham, and
    Melted Cheese, 53
  Ham and Cheese Calzones, 51
  Healthy Beef and Veggie
    Burgers, 61
  Pesto Chicken Pinwheels, 102
  Roasted Broccoli and
    Ricotta Sandwiches, 52
  Smoked Salmon, Avocado,
    and Egg Sandwich
    Pockets, 49
  Tomato and Cheese
    Tortilla Cups, 54
  Tomato Avocado
    Sandwiches, 48
  Turkey, Tomato, and Pesto
    Pita Pockets, 55
  Zucchini and Ham Roll-Ups, 50
Sauces
  Creamy Pecan Sauce, 141
  Healthy Tomato
    Ketchup, 136
  Roasted Tomato Sauce, 137

Sausage
  Broccoli and Sausage
    Risotto, 129
  Pork and Asparagus Tots
    with Tomato Salad, 116
  Turkey Sausage and
    Zucchini Roll-Ups, 108
Savory Breakfast Cookies, 42
Seeds, 20
Sheet Pan Tilapia with
    Potatoes, Tomatoes,
    and Olives, 94–95
Shrimp, 23
  Shrimp and Avocado
    Salad, 80
  Shrimp-Stuffed Zucchini
    Boats, 87
Skillet Mahi-Mahi with Pesto,
    Tomatoes, and Olives, 85
Skillet Steak with Tomato
    and Olives, 120
Skillet Turkey and Peppers, 109
Smoked Salmon, Avocado, and
    Egg Sandwich Pockets, 49
Smoothies
  Immune-Boosting
    Smoothies, 37
  Peanut Butter and Banana
    Smoothies, 35
  Very Berry Grape
    Smoothies, 34
Snacks, 10
Sole and Bulgur–Stuffed
    Tomatoes, 88–89
Solid foods, 3
Soups
  Cream of Carrot and
    Lentil Soup, 67
  Fennel Leek Soup with
    Parmesan Chips, 66
  Vegetable Minestrone, 65
  Wintry Beef and
    Vegetable Stew, 117
Spaghetti and Zoodles, 72
Spices, 9, 20

Spinach
  Baked Spinach Pasta
    Casserole, 76–77
  Cheesy Beef and Spinach
    Baked Pasta, 126
  Fish Grain Bowl, 92–93
  Green Pancakes with
    Blueberries, 41
  Polenta Pizza Squares, 58
  Stir-Fried Beef and
    Spinach, 118
  Super Green Frittata Bread, 43
  Vegetable Minestrone, 65
Squash. *See also* Zucchini
  Beef and Zucchini Baked
    Samosas, 56–57
  Parmesan Roasted Asparagus
    and Butternut Squash, 71
Stir-Fried Beef and Spinach, 118
Sunflower seeds
  Cream of Carrot and
    Lentil Soup, 67
  Super Green Frittata Bread, 43
Sweeteners, 21
Sweet potatoes
  Fish Grain Bowl, 92–93

T

30 minutes or less
  Almond Cocoa Butter, 142
  Apple Rosemary Meatballs
    with Parmesan Cauliflower
    Mash, 122–123
  Apricot Chia Jam, 143
  Asparagus Hummus, 135
  Avocado Yogurt Dip, 134
  Bacon, Sweet Pea, and
    Mushroom Macaroni, 121
  Baked Salmon with Asparagus
    and Mushrooms, 86
  Bowties with Chicken
    and Peas, 106
  Carrot Mayo, 139
  Chocolaty Zucchini
    Oatmeal, 38

Creamy Pecan Sauce, 141
Cucumber, Tomato, Mango,
    and Avocado Salad, 69
Easy Phyllo Pizzas, 59
Eggplant, Tomato, and
    Feta Pasta, 74
Green Deviled Eggs, 33
Green Pancakes with
    Blueberries, 41
Ham and Kale
    Dumplings, 130–131
Healthy Beef and Veggie
    Burgers, 61
Immune-Boosting
    Smoothie, 37
Orange Quinoa Energy
    Bites, 32
Pancetta and Provolone
    Pork Rolls, 127
Peanut Butter and Banana
    Smoothie, 35
Pink Almond Waffles, 40
Polenta Pizza Squares, 58
Pork and Asparagus Tots
    with Tomato Salad, 116
Purple Cabbage
    Potato Salad, 70
Quinoa Chicken Bites, 103
Salmon and Broccoli Fusilli, 83
Salmon and Zucchini
    Skewers, 91
Savory Breakfast Cookies, 42
Shrimp and Avocado Salad, 80
Skillet Mahi-Mahi with Pesto,
    Tomatoes, and Olives, 85
Skillet Steak with Tomato
    and Olives, 120
Smoked Salmon, Avocado, and
    Egg Sandwich Pockets, 49
Stir-Fried Beef and
    Spinach, 118
Tomato and Cheese
    Tortilla Cups, 54
Tomato Avocado
    Sandwiches, 48

Tuna Panzanella, 81
Turkey, Tomato, and Pesto
    Pita Pockets, 55
Turkey Sausage and
    Zucchini Roll-Ups, 108
Very Berry Grape
    Smoothies, 34
Whole-Grain Banana French
    Toast Sticks, 45
Zucchini and Ham Roll-Ups, 50
Zucchini Pesto, 140
Thyme
    Eggplant, Tomato, and
        Feta Pasta, 74
    Fennel Leek Soup with
        Parmesan Chips, 66
    Roasted Tomato Sauce, 137
    Tomato and Cheese
        Tortilla Cups, 54
Toddlers, 3
    eating encouragement
        tips, 10–11
    feeding FAQ, 8–9
    nutritional needs, 4–6
    and picky eating, 7
Tomato and Cheese
    Tortilla Cups, 54
Tomato Avocado
    Sandwiches, 48
Tomatoes, 13
    Bowties with Chicken
        and Peas, 106
    Cod and Zucchini
        Shells Pasta, 84
    Cucumber, Tomato, Mango,
        and Avocado Salad, 69
    Easy Phyllo Pizzas, 59
    Eggplant, Tomato, and
        Feta Pasta, 74
    Healthy Beef and Veggie
        Burgers, 61
    Healthy Tomato Ketchup, 136
    Polenta Pizza Squares, 58
    Pork and Asparagus Tots
        with Tomato Salad, 116

Roasted Broccoli and
    Ricotta Sandwiches, 52
Roasted Chicken and
    Vegetable Quinoa
    Salad, 98–99
Roasted Tomato Sauce, 137
Sheet Pan Tilapia with
    Potatoes, Tomatoes,
    and Olives, 94–95
Skillet Mahi-Mahi with
    Pesto, Tomatoes,
    and Olives, 85
Skillet Turkey and
    Peppers, 109
Sole and Bulgur–Stuffed
    Tomatoes, 88–89
Spaghetti and Zoodles, 72
Tomato and Cheese
    Tortilla Cups, 54
Tomato Avocado
    Sandwiches, 48
Tuna Panzanella, 81
Turkey, Tomato, and Pesto
    Pita Pockets, 55
Turkey Sausage and
    Zucchini Roll-Ups, 108
Tools, 25–26
Tuna Panzanella, 81
Turkey
    Creamy Coconut and
        Turmeric Turkey, 113
    Skillet Turkey and
        Peppers, 109
    Turkey, Tomato, and Pesto
        Pita Pockets, 55
    Turkey Sausage and
        Zucchini Roll-Ups, 108

V

Vegan
    Apricot Chia Jam, 143
    Asparagus Hummus, 135
    Carrot Mayo, 139
    Chocolaty Zucchini
        Oatmeal, 38

Vegan (Continued)
  Cream of Carrot and
    Lentil Soup, 67
  Cucumber, Tomato, Mango,
    and Avocado Salad, 69
  Healthy Tomato
    Ketchup, 136
  Orange Quinoa Energy
    Bites, 32
  Purple Cabbage
    Potato Salad, 70
  Red Lentil and Vegetable
    Bowl, 73
  Roasted Tomato Sauce, 137
  Vegetable Minestrone, 65
Vegetable Minestrone, 65
Vegetables, 6, 63. See also
    specific
  hiding, 18
Vegetarian. See also Vegan
  Almond Cocoa Butter, 142
  Avocado Yogurt Dip, 134
  Baked Spinach Pasta
    Casserole, 76–77
  Blueberry Yogurt Cake, 44
  Broccoli Risotto, 75
  Creamy Pecan Sauce, 141
  Easy Phyllo Pizzas, 59
  Eggplant, Tomato, and
    Feta Pasta, 74
  Fennel Leek Soup with
    Parmesan Chips, 66
  Green Deviled Eggs, 33
  Green Pancakes with
    Blueberries, 41

  Immune-Boosting
    Smoothies, 37
  Mixed-Berry Chia Pudding, 39
  Parmesan Roasted Asparagus
    and Butternut Squash, 71
  Peanut Butter and Banana
    Smoothies, 35
  Pink Almond Waffles, 40
  Polenta Pizza Squares, 58
  Quinoa Veggie Croquettes, 64
  Roasted Broccoli and
    Ricotta Sandwiches, 52
  Spaghetti and Zoodles, 72
  Super Green Frittata Bread, 43
  Tomato and Cheese
    Tortilla Cups, 54
  Very Berry Grape
    Smoothies, 34
  Whole-Grain Banana French
    Toast Sticks, 45
  Zucchini Pesto, 140
Very Berry Grape Smoothies, 34
Vinegars, 21
Vitamins, 5

W

White fish, 23
Whole-Grain Banana French
  Toast Sticks, 45
Wintry Beef and Vegetable
  Stew, 117

Y

Yogurt. See also Greek yogurt
  Pink Almond Waffles, 40

  Salmon and Broccoli
    Fusilli, 83
  Very Berry Grape
    Smoothies, 34

Z

Zucchini, 13
  Beef and Veggie–Stuffed
    Zucchini, 119
  Beef and Zucchini Baked
    Samosas, 56–57
  Beef and Zucchini Pasta
    Bolognese, 124–125
  Chicken Soup for a
    Cold, 100–101
  Chocolaty Zucchini
    Oatmeal, 38
  Cod and Zucchini
    Shells Pasta, 84
  Easy Phyllo Pizzas, 59
  Healthy Beef and Veggie
    Burgers, 61
  Pesto Chicken Pinwheels, 102
  Quinoa Veggie
    Croquettes, 64
  Salmon and Zucchini
    Skewers, 91
  Shrimp-Stuffed Zucchini
    Boats, 87
  Spaghetti and Zoodles, 72
  Turkey Sausage and
    Zucchini Roll-Ups, 108
  Vegetable Minestrone, 65
  Zucchini and Ham Roll-Ups, 50
  Zucchini Pesto, 140

Acknowledgments

First and foremost, thank you to my husband Albert for always believing in my ideas. Every. Single. Crazy. One. Thank you, love, for supporting BuonaPappa since the beginning with love and patience. You taught me to find my voice. You have always been the most honest and encouraging follower, and you were the first one! Thank you for the many times you took the kids to the park, did the dishes, or folded the laundry while I was writing, editing, and filming. You are the best dad I could have dreamed of for our kids.

To my little monsters, Luca and Alex. You fill every moment of my life with joy. LOL, almost every moment. You make me see life through a totally different and wonderful perspective. Thank you for being my little guinea pigs by eating my continuous cooking experiments and for holding, tasting, mixing, and touching food endlessly for my pictures. You are the driving force behind my recipes. I love you more than you will ever know.

To my mom, my pillar of strength. You are the best mom and grandma a girl could ask for. I love you truly, madly, and deeply. And I will translate this for you ☺.

Without my friend Francesca, this book would never have happened. She told me I had to write the book, the one I have been procrastinating about for years. She gave me the final push and I will be always thankful to her . . . for the book and for a million other reasons.

To Sally, our American grandma, who loves my kids like they were her own, because family doesn't always come from blood, but from the heart. Thank you for always being there for me.

To Giulia and Ceci, for being such enthusiastic and positive supporters of your auntie. I love when we cook together.

To Conny and Vera, for all the playdates you organized to give me more time to write and for the beach aperitifs to cheer me up.

To the entire Callisto Media team who helped me step by step throughout this exciting project. You really made this first-time author experience a smooth and comfortable one.

A final, huge, endless thank you to all my readers, followers, and foodie mamas, the online community without whose support I would not be here. Your feedback, comments, thumbs-ups, and likes encouraged and supported me through the years and gave me the energy to keep going with BuonaPappa for the past eight years. This book is for all of you, thank you!!

About the Author

Barbara Lamperti is the recipe developer, photographer, and video creator behind the popular baby food channel BuonaPappa. She is always looking for new ways to make food fun and interesting for kids.

Originally from Italy, Barbara moved to Los Angeles 11 years ago. When she is not cooking, filming, editing, or developing exciting new recipes, Barbara enjoys outdoor activities with her two boys, Alex and Luca, and her husband, Albert. You can find her every Sunday morning at the local farmers' market with her kids, chatting with the farmers and picking the best local organic produce for her family's weekly meals.

For more recipe inspirations and videos, find her online at
www.BuonaPappa.net
https://www.youtube.com/user/BuonaPappa
https://www.instagram.com/buonapappa/